MAKING CHOICES

SOCIAL PROBLEM-SOLVING SKILLS FOR CHILDREN

Mark W. Fraser

James K. Nash

Maeda J. Galinsky

Kathleen M. Darwin

NASW PRESS

National Association
of Social Workers

Washington, DC

Ruth W. Mayden
MSS, LSW, ACSW
President

Josephine Nieves
MSW, PhD
Executive Director

Cheryl Y. Mayberry, *Director, Member Services and Publications*
Paula L. Delo, *Executive Editor*
January Layman-Wood, *Acquisitions Editor*
Donna Daniels Verdier, *Copy Editor*
Robin Bourjaily, *Proofreader*
Leonard S. Rosenbaum, *Indexer*
Mia Reese-Smith, *Editorial Secretary*

Cover illustration by Elizabeth Wolf, Boise, Idaho
Text illustrations by Pat Morrison, Washington, DC
Design and composition by Weber Design, Alexandria, Virginia
Printed and bound by Batson Printing, Benton Harbor, Michigan

Library of Congress Cataloging-in-Publication Data

Making choices: social problem-solving skills for children / by Mark W. Fraser ...[et al.]
    p. cm.
    Includes bibliographical references and index.
    ISBN 0-87101-323-1
    1. Socialization 2. Social skills in children. I. Fraser, Mark W., 1946-

HQ783 .M24 200
303.3'2-dc21   00-045073

C O N T E N T S

Mark W. Fraser, PhD, MSW, holds the John A. Tate Distinguished Professorship for Children in Need at the School of Social Work, University of North Carolina at Chapel Hill. He directs the Carolina Children's Initiative, an early intervention research project for children with aggressive, antisocial behavior. He has written numerous chapters and articles on risk and resilience, child behavior, child and family services, and research methods. With colleagues, he is the author or editor of five books, including a study of intensive family-centered services and a text on research methods related to family studies. In perhaps his most popular book, *Risk and Resilience in Childhood*, published by NASW Press, he and his colleagues explore ways children prevail over adversity, describing resilience-based perspectives for child maltreatment, school dropout, substance abuse, violence, unwanted pregnancy, and other social problems. Dr. Fraser is the editor of the NASW Practice Resources Series.

James K. Nash, PhD, MSW, is assistant professor at the Graduate School of Social Work, Portland State University, in Portland, Oregon. Prior to beginning the doctoral program at UNC-Chapel Hill, Dr. Nash worked for over ten years with children, adolescents, and their families from diverse cultural and ethnic backgrounds, in educational, recreational, public mental health, and other settings. His specific research interests include prevention of youth violence, promoting successful transition from adolescence to adulthood, quantitative research methods, and intervention research. His dissertation research examined the implementation and short-term effects of the *Making Choices* program in a school-based pilot study.

Maeda J. Galinsky, PhD, MSW, is a Kenan Distinguished Professor at the School of Social Work, University of North Carolina at Chapel Hill. She is a co-principal investigator of the Carolina Children's Initiative. She has published extensively on theory and research pertaining to social group work practice. Her recent publications deal with the design, implementation and evaluation of telephone groups for persons with HIV, leadership of multi-racial groups, use of support groups, the theory of technology-based groups, and a conceptual framework for social work practice using a risk and resiliency perspective.

Kathleen M. Darwin, MSW, worked with Dr. Fraser on the *Making Choices* curriculum as a graduate student. In 1988, Ms. Darwin began her career as a public school teacher before entering the field of children's mental health. From 1997 to 1999, she assisted in the development of the North Carolina foster youth organization, SAY-SO (Strong Able Youth Speaking Out), and later served on its advisory board. Ms. Darwin is now in Philadelphia, where she continues her work at the National Board of Medical Examiners.

Making Choices: Social Problem-Solving Skills for Children is the first volume in the

NASW Practice Resources Series, which presents manuals and handbooks that

provide specific guidance on practice strategies. Across all fields of practice and

practice settings, the books in this series explain promising social work interventions

in rich detail, sometimes on a week-by-week or, even, session-by-session basis. Each

practice resource contains guidelines for tailoring content to the unique cultural,

ethnic, and racial characteristics of clients. Concise, flexible, and current, publications

in the series describe the best available practice strategies for a myriad of challenges

that confront 21st century practitioners.

Mark W. Fraser, PhD, MSW
Series Editor

A C K N O W L E D G M E N T S

This manual was written with generous support from the

Z. Smith Reynolds Foundation; the North Carolina State

Division of Mental Health, Developmental Disabilities, and

Substance Abuse Services; the North Carolina Governor's

Crime Commission; and the University of North Carolina

Center for Injury Prevention. Special thanks to Dr. Nicki R.

Crick, University of Minnesota, and Dr. John E. Lochman,

University of Alabama, for helpful comments on drafts of the

manuscript; thanks also to Dr. Vanessa G. Hodges and Dr.

Katherine M. Dunlap at the University of North Carolina

and Dr. Mark J. MacGowan at Florida International

University for their invaluable feedback and guidance. Many

MSW and PhD students gave us helpful advice in

constructing exercises. In particular, we thank Melissa Haffner

and Geetha Gopalan. Finally, we thank also John A. Tate, Jr.,

whose extraordinary dedication to children inspires us all.

MAKING CHOICES
Social Problem-Solving
Skills for Children

Mark W. Fraser

James K. Nash

Maeda J. Galinsky

Kathleen M. Darwin

School of Social Work
University of North Carolina
at Chapel Hill
301 Pittsboro Street, CB 3550
Chapel Hill, NC 27599

INTRODUCTION

The purpose of the *Making Choices* program is to teach social problem-solving skills to children. The *Making Choices* "curriculum" outlines a specific skill-building program that is designed to help children build enduring friendships, work more productively in groups, and respond positively to new social situations. Children who become more skillful in solving social problems usually improve their ability to establish and maintain relationships with peers and adults. When coupled with other supportive services, these skills often positively affect self-esteem and school behavior.

Making Choices has been used to teach problem solving both to children in general and to children whose behavior is impulsive, oppositional, or aggressive. With minor modifications the content is appropriate for use with children from kindergarten to early middle school, in classroom or small group settings. Each unit and lesson includes ideas on when and how to adapt activities for use with children at different points in social development.

ABOUT SOCIAL PROBLEM SOLVING

Making Choices emphasizes a cognitive problem-solving perspective. It is based on the connections among the ways children think, feel, and act in solving social problems. Across a variety of settings and with numerous peers and adults, children engage in many forms of problem solving. Problem solving may involve simple, quickly resolved issues—for example, whether to play with a ball or hunt for bugs at recess or whether to share crayons or colored pencils with a friend. It may also involve more socially complicated and emotion-filled issues—for example, how to become accepted in a popular peer group or how to avoid conflicts with a bully. Much of children's behavior can be understood as an effort to solve big and little problems in order to get along with others and accomplish personal social goals. Sometimes children's goals are instrumental, as in obtaining the use of a particular toy during a play period, and sometimes their goals are more social or relational, as in establishing friendships or, in the case of bullying, dealing with the domineering behavior of a peer. In this book we focus on how children solve instrumental and relational problems that involve other people, both peers and adults, in various social situations.

Many environmental and developmental factors influence the behavior of children; these factors include individual, family, school, neighborhood, and broad contextual influences (Fraser, 1996a). From an ecological perspective, *Making Choices* addresses individual risk factors, and it may be used as a component of a broader set of services—ones that focus on risk conditions in the family and neighborhood, as well as conditions in the schools—to strengthen supportive systems for children.

Taking into account the range of environmental factors that affect children and families, recent research strongly suggests that cognitive processes play a critical role in shaping behavior (see, for example, Brower & Nurius, 1993; Nurius & Berlin, 1995). This perspective assumes that children (and adults) are exposed to an array of environmental cues when they encounter a social situation. Often automatically, they complete a sequence of cognitive processes before responding with behavior. The manner in which these cognitive processes are completed greatly affects social outcomes, be they instrumental or relational.

The more technical name for these cognitive sequences is *information processing.* The research literature on processing social information is rich (for reviews, see Crick & Dodge, 1994, and Lochman & Lenhart, 1993). In this book we will refer to social information processing as *cognitive problem solving* or simply *problem solving.* Sequenced according to information-processing theory, the *Making Choices* curriculum is designed to teach children to improve their social skills by making more conscious use of cognitive processes.

Social Cues

A cue can be anything a child sees, hears, touches, tastes, or smells. In most social situations, the important cues involve seeing, hearing, and touching (or being touched). Social cues usually come from other people. They include, for example, the words people use, their facial expressions, their body language, and their actions, as well as contextual factors such as the presence or absence of supportive adults. In almost all cases children receive cues from the setting itself. A child might, for example, notice that a friend's room is furnished like his or her own bedroom at home, or that a friend's family eats spicy foods or uses chopsticks to eat dinner. Consider the following situation:

Sadie walks into a busy classroom and sees a peer, Alissa, playing with Sadie's favorite toy. Alissa looks up and at Sadie, smiles, and says, "Good morning."

This situation presents Sadie with several cues. Overt cues include the words that Alissa used, the way she is playing with the toy (is she being careful, or is she doing something that might damage it?), other children playing an active game in the center of the room, a big box of toys, and the teacher sitting at a desk. Less obvious cues include Alissa's tone of voice, two children reading quietly in the corner, and a poster on the wall that lists rules about sharing toys. When children encounter social cues in a situation, whether in the home, in the classroom, or on the street, they usually respond with some sort of behavior. They engage in social problem solving.

Processing Social Cues

According to the cognitive perspective, a child's response to social cues is not a direct consequence of the particular cues encountered. Rather, a sequence of cognitive processes shapes his or her responses (or efforts to problem solve) (Crick & Dodge, 1994). Children's behavior—and perhaps all human behavior—is deeply influenced by the context of and the manner in which the problem-solving sequence occurs. One might ask these questions about the scenario just described: Which cues did Sadie notice when she entered the room? Did she see Alissa smile and hear her say good morning? Does Sadie like or dislike Alissa? Did Sadie see the poster stating the rules about sharing? Did she pay attention to it? Did she see the other children playing a game or the group of children reading in the corner? Did she think about whether she wanted to join them?

In the *Making Choices* approach, Sadie's response is a product of the sequence of cognitive processes that deals with interpreting the social environment within the specific social context at hand. In this sense the interpretation of cues is contextually dependent; that is, a child must learn to assess cues in a given setting. An encounter with a bully on school grounds with a teacher nearby

might produce a different set of behaviors than would a similar encounter occurring on the street. Developing social responses is based on highly subjective social perceptions.[1]

Six Steps in Solving Social Problems

Social problem solving consists of six interrelated information-processing steps, each of which corresponds to a separate unit in the *Making Choices* program:
1. Encoding cues
2. Interpreting cues
3. Formulating and refining social goals
4. Searching for and formulating responses to social situations
5. Deciding on particular responses
6. Enacting or implementing response decisions.

Table 1 (see Appendix) briefly describes each step and Figure 2 (see Appendix) illustrates a single problem-solving sequence. Each unit in *Making Choices* begins with a brief description of one of the problem-solving steps and contains lessons and activities designed to help children learn step-related skills (see below for more on the organization of the curriculum).

In real life, social situations are dynamic, constantly emerging and often becoming

---

[1] This perspective can be contrasted with a behavioral approach, which explains behavior simply as the direct response to a stimulus or cue, unmediated by cognitive processes. Figure 1 (see Appendix) depicts these two approaches to behavior.

more complex. Even when children engage in problem solving in a relatively simple situation, they encounter multiple cues and they must complete, revise, and reinitiate problem-solving sequences. Sequences often overlap in time and occur simultaneously (Crick & Dodge, 1994).

Consequently, we conceptualize problem solving as an iterative and interactive—and certainly nonlinear—process involving feedback and thus constant formulation and reformulation. Although in day-to-day practice, problem solving develops along multiple pathways and is characterized by feedback loops, starts and stops, and midstream reformulation, we use steps to describe the basic elements of problem solving.

Heuristics

For most people, and in most situations, problem solving is also highly automatic. Generally, neither adults nor children actively think about the sequence of cognitive processes that occurs in making social choices. Often, in fact, we rely on what are called *heuristics*. A heuristic is a rule of thumb or, from the perspective of cognitive theory, a preprogrammed set of rules or strategies that determine how social cues are processed. Like a computer program, a heuristic is made up of a series of instructions that automatically process information. Heuristics enable people to process numerous cues, and they require little or

no active effort or awareness (Brower & Nurius, 1993; Nurius & Berlin, 1995).

In many situations automatic processing works well; however, overreliance on heuristics can lead to an inaccurate or incomplete understanding of a situation. For example, an important step in the problem-solving sequence involves assigning meaning to, or interpreting, a social cue. One common heuristic for accomplishing this is simply to assign the first meaning that comes to mind. This is often called the *availability heuristic* (Dawes, 1988).

Figure 3 depicts how the availability heuristic operates to automate the cognitive process of interpretation. Once a cue has been encoded, the heuristic is activated. A typical sequence might consist of the following steps:

- Observe the setting and encode social cues.
- Access the first available idea that comes to mind.
- Assign meaning to cues based on the first idea.
- Ignore other, and possibly conflicting, cues. Disregard alternative meanings of encoded cues.
- Make interpretation.

The availability heuristic requires little effort, and in many cases it would probably be accurate enough. However, in some situations its use would almost certainly result in an inaccurate assignment of meaning to relevant cues.

This misreading could, in turn, adversely affect the quality of a social interaction and lead to a poor outcome—conflict, social rejection, being viewed as a bully, and so on. For example:

James walks into the classroom one morning to find another boy, Louis, putting together the puzzle James was planning to use. Without looking up, Louis asks James if he wants to help with the puzzle.

Consider one way James might interpret the situation when he sees Louis. Suppose James has a younger sister who just this morning broke his best toy truck. This incident is still fresh in his mind and, when he sees Louis, the first thought that comes to him is: "Uh-oh. Louis is playing with the farm puzzle and I love that puzzle. He's sure to mess it up if he keeps playing with it, just like my dumb sister, and I'll never get to use it again!"

Use of the availability heuristic automatically leads to an interpretation that is based solely on first thoughts. Often, these first thoughts concern our most recent experiences. James fails to formulate competing interpretations and does not use additional information to assign meaning to what he sees. That is, he does not notice, attend to, or interpret any other cues present in the situation, such as Louis's offer to let him help with the puzzle. Therefore, James may adopt a social strategy designed to obtain control of the puzzle. Because of poor encoding and interpretation skills, James ignores goals and behaviors that would elicit sharing or taking turns. Instead, he elects a coercive strategy that may produce a short-run gain— possession of the puzzle—and a long-run loss—being disliked by Louis.

Another heuristic that people often use is the representative heuristic. Representative thinking involves interpreting one cue in terms of how much it is like another cue (Dawes, 1988; Tversky & Kahneman, 1983). For example, suppose James and Louis had fought over a different game twice during the previous week. When James sees Louis playing with this puzzle, James might process what he sees like this: "Oh no, Louis is playing with that puzzle I wanted. He always gets to the things I want before I do! Just like with that game last week—he got to play with it every time I wanted it last week. I never get to play with what I want!" In contrast to the first example of how James might react, this interpretation might not be the first thing that comes to James's mind. He might notice other toys and other children, and he might also see the teacher watching him. Seeing Louis with the puzzle is such a powerful reminder of what happened the previous week, however, that an interpretation representative of a recent event prevails. Here again the process is automatic and leads to a distorted interpretation that could lead to conflict.[2]

---

[2] Recall that Louis indicated he was willing to share.

The Problem with Heuristics

As mentioned above, our minds use heuristics to process information all the time, and very often heuristics work well. They require little or no active effort. Shaped by our prior experiences, they are efficient and allow us to process the vast amount of information we encounter daily. And in problem-free social interactions, they often result in quite accurate interpretations of social cues. Their use becomes problematic, however, whenever they produce inaccurate interpretations and conflict. As one might expect, it is particularly problematic (and possibly dangerous) when the use of heuristics leads children to interpret potentially hazardous situations as benign or attractive. And vice versa: If a child has learned to interpret the behavior of adults as potentially dangerous, he or she is likely to view teachers, school counselors, social workers, and others as hostile in intent. This can get in the way of establishing positive relationships with adults and peers of good will. In short, what may be functional in one context may not be functional in another context.

The use of heuristics implies automatic processing of social cues. James did not make a conscious decision to interpret the situation based on the first thought that came to mind, or because the situation resembled another incident. Instead, his mind automatically processed the cue he received, by means of a heuristic, and this led to a specific interpretation. The use of automatic processing in these examples is likely to result in inferior problem solving.

We have emphasized how reliance on automatic processing can lead to inaccurate or distorted interpretations of social cues and to conflict. But what happens if children do not rely solely on automatic processing? What if they *stop and think* about what is going on?

TEACHING CHILDREN TO STOP AND THINK

An important idea behind the *Making Choices* curriculum is that children, even young children, can learn how information processing affects their behavior. Instead of relying solely on automatic processing, they can learn about problem solving—that is, about *Making Choices*. Children with strong problem-solving skills often are better-liked by peers and judged by teachers to be less aggressive than children who display deficient skills (Ladd & Price, 1986; Lochman et al., 1993; Pettit, Dodge, & Brown, 1988). By gaining insight into social processes and by learning to identify and formulate alternatives at each step of the information-processing sequence, children can learn to make and keep friends, to interact with adults in rewarding ways, and to assess potential risks or threats in social circumstances more quickly. By using mindful rather than automatic processing, they can learn to respond to a wide variety of social cues, to interpret those cues more accurately, and to adopt social strategies that will enhance their ability to function more successfully in a variety of settings. As children gain confidence in their ability to use these strategies, they form the building blocks of successful relationships in the home, in school, and, later, in the world of work (see, for example, Bandura, 1993). The development and refinement of these skills is the goal of the *Making Choices* program.

Making Choices focuses on each step of the problem-solving sequence and teaches children how to think before they act. An integral component of normal social development, this approach is especially appropriate for children who are impulsive, oppositional, or easily swayed by their peers into negative behavior. A great deal of research describes the ways in which the cognitive processing skills of these children differ from, and lag behind, those of other children (for a review, see Fraser, 1996b). We will briefly describe and use some of this research in each unit.

A Feeling and Thinking Perspective

This curriculum also emphasizes how the emotional state of a child influences social problem solving. Some children, because they have poor cognitive skills, simply don't know how to think about problem solving (Kendall, 1993). Others could, but their lives are disturbed by the stress and disorder of poverty, of dangerous neighborhoods, of child abuse, or of other contextual factors that dampen creativity, sour relationships, and crush hope (Graham, Hudley, & Williams, 1992; Guerra et al., 1995).[3] The cultural background and family history of a child, as well as situationally specific factors, such as setting or time of day, may also affect a child's capacity to use particular cognitive problem-solving skills. Although it is not feasible to address the implications of all such factors in the curriculum, we encourage group leaders to keep them in mind when leading a *Making Choices* group. You can modify the content to address cultural, developmental, and setting-specific factors as needed (see Cartledge, Lee, & Feng, 1995). We sometimes suggest ideas for addressing a particular factor and its effects on a selected step of the problem-solving sequence.[4]

---

[3] Under these conditions, *Making Choices* is by itself an insufficient intervention. It should be viewed as one element of a multi-component intervention that addresses the wide range of individual, family, school, and neighborhood risk factors affecting children. For a review of promising family, school, neighborhood and other interventions, see Fraser (1996a).

We have chosen to include in the curriculum a unit that examines the influence of one especially important factor: the emotional state of a child during a social situation. Practice experience and research have shown that this factor often has a profound effect on children's problem solving and resulting behavior (Crick & Dodge, 1994; Graham, Hudley, & Williams, 1992; Lochman & Dodge, 1994). The term emotional state refers to the feelings a child is experiencing and to the affect he or she displays in a specific social situation. It also refers to more enduring characteristics, such as an overall tendency to be cheerful (or sad, angry, and so on), specific psychological diagnoses (depression, for example), or typical ways of reacting (for example, "easily angered").

We introduce material about feelings and describe related activities at the beginning of *Making Choices*. In the first unit children learn about the range of feelings people experience, how to identify feelings in themselves and others, and how feelings may relate to specific situations. They learn about strategies for recognizing and regulating their own feelings, and, through activities, games, and stories, they practice applying these concepts.

In subsequent units children continue to explore concepts and develop skills for dealing with feelings. As the content of the *Making Choices* program unfolds, they apply these concepts and skills to each step of the problem-solving sequence.

Overt and Relational Aggression

Over the past several years, researchers have begun to hypothesize the existence of two principal types of childhood aggression: *overt* and *relational* (see, for example, Crick, 1995: Crick & Grotpeter, 1995). Overt aggression refers to behaviors that use or threaten force—hitting, kicking, or shoving, for example —with the intent of causing physical harm. Relational aggression, in contrast, includes actions such as excluding a peer from an activity or group, spreading rumors, or refusing to talk to a peer. Although these actions do not result in physical harm, the intent to do harm—to cause damage to peer relationships—is nevertheless present. Hence the name, relational aggression. The appropriateness of labeling such actions "aggressive" may be debatable, but the research evidence showing that sizable numbers of children engage in these behaviors is fairly strong.

---

[4] This curriculum is distinguished by reliance on research that has included adequate samples of African-American children. The problem-solving sequence is known to have wide applicability. However, trainers will need to adapt ideas and create examples that reflect current issues and pressures in different children's lives.

Research also indicates that there may be a correlation between gender and the use of relational aggression (Crick, 1995; Crick & Grotpeter, 1995). Although many children who use overt aggression also use relational aggression, and while boys tend to be more aggressive overall, girls may be somewhat more likely to engage in relational aggression. Evidence is also emerging that relationally aggressive behaviors are perceived by other children as hurtful (Crick & Grotpeter, 1996), that their use may be predictive of social maladjustment (Crick, 1996), and that deficits in social information-processing increase the likelihood that children will engage in relational aggression (Crick & Wellman, 1997). Thus, relational aggression represents a potentially serious problem for many children. The *Making Choices* program is suitable for its prevention and treatment, and we therefore include material on relational aggression throughout the manual.

Reactive and Proactive Aggression

Researchers have also identified two subtypes of overt aggression, *reactive* and *proactive* aggression. Although both involve real or threatened physical harm, they differ in some important ways. Reactive aggression occurs under conditions of high emotion, such as when children are angry or fearful. Children who are reactively aggressive are often impulsive and have attention

problems. They hit, kick, or punch other children in social situations without thinking much, or at all, about the consequences of their actions.

In contrast, proactive aggression is a planned strategy, performed with the aim of attaining a particular goal. Anger or fear play little or no role in proactive aggression. Children who are proactively aggressive have usually thought about what is going on in a social situation, they have formulated a goal, and they have decided that physical force is the best way to reach that goal.

As might be expected, deficits in information-processing are thought to play a role in reactive and proactive aggression. Hostile attribution bias—attributing hostile intent to others even if it is not there—and errors in encoding cues are linked with reactive aggression. Reactively aggressive children may notice only a limited number of cues in a situation and impulsively label these hostile. They may become quickly angered and seek to strike out, without paying attention to additional cues or coming up with alternative interpretations. Proactive aggression, in contrast, appears to be the result of children's judgment that aggressive actions will more likely help them reach a goal than would other behavioral strategies. They might make this evaluation simply because prosocial responses do not occur to these children, or perhaps they lack confidence in their ability to carry out a prosocial response or think that a prosocial response would be ineffective in helping them reach their goal.

Many children engage in both proactive and reactive aggression. So far, researchers have not identified reactive and proactive forms of relational aggression, although that distinction may hold for this type of aggression as well.

Problem Solving and Violence in Context

Making Choices is designed to give children alternative ways to think about social situations and to formulate social goals and responses. An important goal of this curriculum is to teach children ways to interact with others in a peaceful, nonaggressive manner. Yet many children come from dangerous neighborhoods and have learned that they have to be tough to survive, and being tough often means looking and being aggressive. Moreover, many have been exposed to adult problem solving that employs coercion and violence. When leading a *Making Choices* group, we believe it is counterproductive to emphasize the single perspective that fighting is wrong in any situation. Many children who might benefit from the *Making Choices* program might find such a message puzzling, if not irrelevant.

We argue that it is more effective to teach children that they always have choices about how they act (Larson,

1994). When children stop and think before acting, research suggests, they will produce behavior that is more likely to get them what they want and need (Lochman, 1992). Moreover, they are less likely to adopt a strategy that will get them into trouble, and more likely to produce behavior that does not result in anyone getting hurt (for reviews of this research, see Kendall, 1993; Lochman & Lenhart, 1993).

We encourage group leaders to give children some version of the following message:

> *Thinking actively about what's going on in a situation, and about all the ways you might accomplish your goals, is a powerful way to get what you really want. You can use the skills you learn in* Making Choices *to make good friends; to improve your relationships with teachers, coaches, and family members; and to become a leader in your group or school.*

THE UNIQUENESS OF THE *MAKING CHOICES* CURRICULUM

Teachers, social workers, counselors, and other professionals who work with children are probably well aware of the existence of numerous training curricula to improve problem-solving and social interaction skills. Among others, these include the Anger Coping Program (Lochman et al., 1987), Second Step (Grossman et al., 1997), *The Prepare Curriculum* (Goldstein, 1988), and

Bloomquist's (1996) *Skills Training for Children with Behavior Deficits.* Although *Making Choices* resembles these curricula in several ways (by drawing from a similar conceptual perspective, for example, or by incorporating comparable activities), it is a significant departure from other skills-training programs. Unlike those programs, *Making Choices* focuses on a sequence of selected problem-solving skills that have been empirically demonstrated to relate to aggression and other indicators of social maladjustment in children.[5] This sequence is deeply rooted in research that includes studies of African-American and other minority children. Moreover, the sequence appears equally adaptive for overt and relational aggression.

The Social Information-Processing Model

Our curriculum draws directly from the work of Crick and Dodge (1994), whose model of the social information-processing (SIP) sequence was described above. This model breaks down the problem-solving sequence into several well-defined "individual cognitive tasks that might be involved when a child is engaged in social interaction" (p. 74). *Making Choices* is unique in that it addresses each step in the SIP sequence

and emphasizes the development of those skills that, according to recent research, show a high correlation with social adjustment. For example, the SIP model emphasizes the importance of, and robust support for, the connection between hostile attribution bias and aggression. In the unit on interpretation (unit 3), *Making Choices* devotes extensive time to this issue, with activities explicitly designed to teach children skills for improving the accuracy of their interpretation of others' intentions. Similarly, *Making Choices* conceptualizes social goals in a manner consistent with the SIP model. Our emphasis on teaching children to distinguish helpful and harmful goals follows directly from several studies that found a relationship between formulation of prosocial goals and social adjustment. Other examples are those activities in *Making Choices* that teach children to formulate multiple responses in a social situation, as well as to carefully evaluate the nature of each response (for example, Is it harmful or helpful? Is the child confident that he or she can enact the response?).

Perhaps most importantly, *Making Choices* reflects the proposition that information processing of a single cue or stimulus in a social situation occurs sequentially and that each step of the

---

[5] To date, most research on social information-processing and aggression in children has focused on overt aggression in males. Some studies do include small numbers of girls, and recently several researchers have included large numbers of girls in their samples. In describing research results, we have tried to note when samples included boys only and to report any gender-related differences.

sequence can influence subsequent steps, and, consequently, the behavioral response of a child (Crick & Dodge, 1994). Although social interaction within a particular situation usually involves completion of multiple, overlapping information-processing sequences (*simultaneous processing*), we focus on teaching children how to complete each constituent step in the sequence successfully. By emphasizing each step in the SIP sequence, *Making Choices* aims to improve a variety of cognitive skills that appear to be strongly related to competence in problem solving with peers and adults.

However, *Making Choices* differs from the social information-processing model in a number of ways. These differences are minor and, we believe, represent refinements that often occur as one attempts to operationalize theory in the applied world of intervention. For example, *Making Choices* provides an explicit definition for a social problem during the interpretation step of information processing. The term *problem* was not well defined in the SIP model (Crick & Dodge, 1994); we define it in unit 3 in order to organize concepts and to provide a focus for subsequent learning activities. In unit 6, "Response Selection," *Making Choices* sets out activities to teach children to evaluate potential responses on dimensions that were not explicitly described in the SIP model. We define *response evaluation* to include an

assessment of how well a potential response fits a particular social situation, and whether the response will help a child reach a selected goal.

Although the social information-processing model informs this curriculum by providing an explanatory framework for understanding childhood aggression and by suggesting targets for sequenced intervention, *Making Choices* utilizes learning activities that are not described in the SIP model. For example, in developing the social information-processing model, Crick and Dodge (1994) distinguished cognitive outputs (that is, *what* children think) and cognitive processes (that is, *how* children think), and noted that most research deals with the former. Hostile attribution bias is an example of a cognitive output, one that research has shown to be associated with aggression. However, for the most part, research has not yet examined the cognitive processes by which aggressive children arrive at a biased attribution in social situations (for example, by interpreting a cue using a heuristic or by attempting to evaluate a peer's intent based on a sequence of cues). *Making Choices*, in contrast, contains many activities designed to teach children how to complete cognitive processes in a manner that will produce socially competent cognitive output. Similarly, no research to date has examined when, and under what circumstances, children access potential responses from memory (thinking of a response they have completed or seen before) and when they construct new strategies. In *Making Choices*, we encourage children to use both approaches to response formulation, without assuming that one approach will necessarily produce more socially competent responses.

Making Choices and The Anger Coping Program

The Anger Coping Program (ACP) developed by John Lochman and his colleagues has also greatly influenced *Making Choices*, both conceptually and technically (Lochman et al., 1987). Conceptually, the ACP and related research draw from, and have contributed much to, the social cognitive and social information-processing perspective. A number of basic concepts and skills taught in the ACP appear in *Making Choices*. These include goal setting and response formulation (or *generating alternatives*). Technically, we also owe much to the methods described by Lochman and associates (1987) and elsewhere (for example, Lochman, Dunn, & Klimes-Dougan, 1993; Lochman & Lenhart, 1993). For example, *Making Choices* teaches techniques such as self-talk, which is an important component of the ACP. We also teach skills via similar technology, that is, the use of audiotapes and videotapes to help children practice concepts and skills presented in the group. And we have incorporated certain

contextualizing features described in the ACP into this curriculum, such as the importance of collaboration with parents and teachers and the need to have group participants set a "real-life" behavioral goal to gain practice in applying problem-solving concepts outside of the group setting.

At the same time, *Making Choices* differs from the ACP in several important ways. First, and most important, our detailed focus on each step of the social information-processing sequence, as described above, represents a significant departure from the ACP. The ACP curriculum emphasizes anger control and conceptualizes the problem-solving sequence as problem recognition, goal setting, generating alternatives, and identifying consequences, without emphasizing the earliest steps in the SIP sequence, encoding, and interpretation of cues (Lochman et al., 1987). We also introduce and teach content on a wide array of emotions, while the ACP focuses on the role of a single emotion, anger, in social interactions. Throughout the *Making Choices* program, children are encouraged to think about the competing influences of a variety of emotions as they engage in the steps of social problem solving. Further, *Making Choices* is adaptable for use with children from early elementary through early middle school. We include numerous activities designed to help children understand the meaning of important basic concepts (for example, social cue, intent, problem, goal) and provide examples of how to phrase definitions to suit the developmental level of group members. Thus, *Making Choices* has wide application for both early intervention and prevention. Finally, this program manual includes an introductory section designed to help group leaders develop positive group interactions and productive group process, and to structure and implement a proactive behavior management system.

LEADING *MAKING CHOICES* GROUPS: NOTES FOR GROUP LEADERS

The Need for Collaboration: An Ecological Perspective

Children's behavior in one setting is influenced by what goes on in other settings (see, for example, Dishion & Andrews, 1995; Dodge, Bates, & Pettit, 1990; Pettit et al., 1988; Sheline, Skipper, & Broadhead, 1994; Tolan, Guerra, & Kendall, 1995). Life at home affects how a child functions at school. School performance influences the child's functioning after school. The after-school experience has an impact on life at home. And neighborhood conditions influence the family and school, shaping activities, beliefs, and opportunities. The skills learned from *Making Choices* can help a child negotiate relationships at home, in school, and in the community.

In order to build this perspective into the curriculum, partnerships with parents and teachers and other important figures in a child's life must be developed. The outcomes of *Making Choices* are likely to be better if group leaders meet with parents and teachers to explain the purpose of the program (see, for example, Lochman & Lenhart, 1993). Parents and teachers can provide critical information about a child's strengths at home and in the classroom. In addition, they may have specific suggestions about the areas in which a child should concentrate efforts. Group leaders should maintain regular contact with teachers and parents. Throughout the course of *Making Choices*, leaders should keep teachers and parents updated on the concepts and skills that students are learning. Attempt to enlist parents' and teachers' support in encouraging students to practice new skills during the week. Encourage students to seek the input of their parents and teachers when setting personal behavioral goals.

To monitor the students' progress towards goals, establish a means of regular written communication between group leaders and the classroom or home. The degree to which *Making Choices* has an impact may be related to parent and teacher involvement in and support of children's efforts to use problem-solving skills in daily life. After the conclusion of the *Making Choices* program, periodic follow-up meetings with parents, teachers, and group members are recommended. Research suggests that "booster shots" of support and supplemental training produce longer-lasting treatment effects (Dishion & Andrews, 1995).

Screening Potential Members Of Making Choices Groups

As mentioned above, the *Making Choices* program has been designed for use in regular classrooms, as primary prevention, as well as a targeted intervention in small groups of children who are experiencing difficulty in social interactions. Research suggests that skills learned in *Making Choices* are likely to help all children function more easily in social settings (Crick & Dodge, 1994). Thus, as primary prevention, the program is appropriate for use in mainstream classrooms of students from kindergarten to early middle school. As a targeted intervention, specific screening criteria are useful for identifying children who may be experiencing deficits in the kinds of problem-solving skills taught in *Making Choices*. We use a two-step screening process.

First, *Making Choices* is designed for children between six and 13 years of age, who have no serious physical impairment, intellectual deficit, or behavior disorder that requires placement outside a regular classroom. Second, children are defined as at-risk if they manifest developmentally inappropriate aggressive or disruptive behavior in the classroom or other settings and if they are isolated from or

rejected by other children. There is considerable evidence that frequent use of aggression and rejection by peers is an indicator that a child has embarked on a trajectory of negative behavior that, without intervention, may lead to academic failure, delinquency, substance use, and other negative developmental outcomes (Fraser, 1996a).

Research evidence also suggests that groups composed entirely of at-risk students can produce harmful outcomes (Dishion & Andrews, 1995; Feldman, Caplinger, & Wodarski, 1983). When used as a targeted intervention with children identified as at-risk, it is essential, we believe, that *Making Choices* groups include a mix of at-risk students and students who display positive and prosocial problem-solving skills. Furthermore, we recommend that prosocial students make up the majority of group members. Though we are still collecting and analyzing research data, even quite skillful children appear to benefit from the *Making Choices* program. Students— whether at-risk or not—learn skills that will help them be more successful in negotiating social situations both in school and in the home.

Organization of the Making Choices Program

The curriculum begins with a section that sets out suggestions and guidelines for working with children's groups ("Getting Started"). The remainder of

Making Choices consists of the seven instructional units. Except for unit 1 ("The Role of Emotions"), each unit corresponds to one of the six steps in the cognitive problem-solving sequence. Each unit begins with a brief definition of the step in the sequence, along with a research-based description of how the skills of children who are aggressive may be deficient at that juncture.

Each unit contains three to five lessons. An explicit goal guides the lessons and activities of each unit, and every lesson has a specific objective. We recommend that, during the early sessions, group leaders plan to cover a single lesson each time the group meets. As you get to know the children in your group (or class) and become more familiar with the content, you may be able to cover multiple lessons during a single session.

We also recommend that the program be presented by two coleaders. An ideal team would consist of a person with expertise in mental health and a person with experience in schools, such as a guidance counselor or school social worker. Having two leaders provides more effective group management and helps in managing the logistics of many activities. In addition, the school-based professional can be a great asset in establishing and maintaining positive collaborative relationships with teachers, and the mental health worker might take responsibility for developing parent partnerships.

WORKING WITH GROUPS

The *Making Choices* program is designed for a group setting. Therefore, leaders should be familiar with the way groups develop and with ways to facilitate the effective use of groups. It is especially important that you consider group characteristics in your planning of group activities. Whether in large groups such as school classrooms or in small groups such as those that might be offered by an after-school program, group discussion and group interaction are important components of *Making Choices*. As the children work together on activities, their experiences with one another will be crucial to learning content and acquiring skills for achieving the lesson objectives.

Although groups of children differ, there are some general principles of group leadership that may be helpful in implementing the *Making Choices* curriculum. It is useful to have knowledge of group process and group development so that you know what to expect as children work from lesson to lesson. This knowledge informs you about what you can do to facilitate the group's interactions and accomplishments. Our brief review of group development will alert you to some important features of groups at different stages of development. It will point to issues to consider as you go through the *Making Choices* program with your group, whether the group is

16

large or small. We have emphasized concepts related to group goals, bonds, roles, and norms. A more comprehensive treatment of group principles and practices can be found in Garvin (1997); Kelly and Berman-Rossi (1999); Rose (1998); and Toseland and Rivas (1998). More information about frameworks of group development can be found in Brower (1996); Galinsky and Schopler (1989); Garland, Jones, and Kolodny (1976); Sarri and Galinsky (1985); Tuckman and Jensen (1977); Wheelan and Kaeser (1997); and Worchel (1994).

Planning: The Origin Phase

Before the group even meets, try to anticipate those factors that might promote its growth. We refer to this as the *origin* or *planning phase* of group development. You will want to consider the environment in which the group will be located. What can you do to create a physical setting that promotes positive interaction among members? Movable chairs that you can arrange in a circle, for example, may promote interaction. Having adequate space, free from distractions, can enhance the ability of group members to concentrate and carry out activities. Then, too, you may want to think about the group's "mood" when members assemble. Where will they have been just before arriving at the group meeting—sitting in a math class, eating lunch, or having free time on the playground? Where will they be going

after the meeting—to the cafeteria, the gym, an after-school program, or home? Is this true for all group members? Might any recent incident have influenced how the students interact with one another? What discipline issues could arise?

Furthermore, the composition and size of the group will affect how you plan activities. If *Making Choices* takes place in a regular classroom setting with a large number of participants, you will want to consider ways to pair children or use smaller groups for practice and discussion. If the group is composed of both children who are at-risk and those who are not, you will want to take this into account as you create subgroups or pairs. The activities you choose will, of course, depend on the ages and abilities of the group members.

Building Relationships and Expectations: The Forming Phase

When members first assemble in what we call the *forming* phase, they begin to get acquainted with one another as a group. They learn about what is expected of them in this particular group, the goals or purposes and the rules of the group, and how the group operates. As participants join the group, they are bound to question what the experience will be like for them. Will they belong? Will the others group members like them? Will the others understand them? Will they get something out of the group? It's hard for students to pay attention to the lessons and activities, and to what others are saying, if they are worrying about their own place in the group.

What you do at the beginning of the group helps set the tone for the rest of the group sessions. Trust building and enhancing member security are important at this phase. Thus, it is critical to put students at ease, to ensure that they know they have a place in the group, and to connect them in a positive way to one another. In this phase, and in others as well, the "go-around" format may be especially helpful. In this format, each individual has a turn to tell something specific, so that everyone is included and no one feels left out. From the beginning, do whatever you can to help develop the group—member interactions and mutual aid are important components of the *Making Choices* program. It is especially important at this beginning phase that you tell members the objectives of the program, what rules they have to follow, how you expect them to treat others, what their responsibilities are in terms of attendance and participation, and what they can hope to gain from the group. For example, rules of "no put-downs" and "no laughing at another's attempts to problem solve," plus expectations for giving positive feedback to each other, might be established early. Encourage members to suggest rules and to think of how they will take responsibility for

monitoring them. Also, draw members into the goal-setting process. Member ownership of and commitment to the group can be powerful forces. And remember, whatever takes place with any individual in the group—for example, how you as leader interact with a particular student—takes place within the context of the group and communicates to other members how they will be treated. In addition, when there are coleaders, their relationship and interactions serve as models for members.

Testing: The Storming Phase

Once members move beyond the forming stage, they begin to feel more comfortable and secure. They may begin to engage in more conflictual interactions with each other. Typically, too, they begin to question the goals and operations of the group and the authority of the group leader. This has been called the *storming* phase, or power and control phase. Of course, with children who have difficulty with aggression, this type of testing may occur from the very beginning of group meetings, and it may be based more on personal rather than group characteristics. In some types of groups, group leaders seek to nurture (or even encourage) this storming phase to aid the group's ability to deal with disagreements and to develop its independence. However, for most *Making Choices* groups, it is important that the leader modulate the expression of conflict and keep the storming within bounds. At the same

18

time, instances of conflict, such as testing the leader or arguing with another group member, may be used to illustrate and reinforce the use of problem-solving skills. If two members are about to get into a serious altercation, the leader might point out the need to encode all of the cues in the situation or to interpret accurately what is going on.

Working Together: The Performing Phase

The next two phases of the group, which we will treat here as a single phase, are termed *norming* and *performing*. At this stage, many of the problems of the group's functioning have been worked out and the group has developed at least a moderate amount of cohesion. Norms are clear and members know what is expected of them in terms of performance. Members may function fairly independently of a leader's guidance. Given the structured format of *Making Choices* groups (and given that some children in *Making Choices* groups may be prone to disruptive or oppositional behavior), the leader will want to remain in charge of the group process, even at this stage of group development. This will mean guiding the group with a firm hand through the educational part of the curriculum and through the practice activities.

Although children in *Making Choices* groups may not be able to contribute

equally, leaders should involve the students as much as possible in the group process and ensure that they develop ownership for group functioning, including the development of a mutual aid climate. The groups are designed so that children can provide support and assistance to one another as they explore feelings, learn new skills, and solve interpersonal problems. It is important for members to take responsibility for group solutions, to enforce rules, and to help one another reach individual goals. Because many of the activities of the curriculum take place through member interactions, the more the group can be developed and utilized, the greater will be the impact on children's problem-solving skills.

Evaluating and Ending: The Termination Phase

The final phase is *termination*. As the group ends, children talk about their accomplishments, end their personal attachments to the group, and make transitions from what they have learned to other parts of their lives. Although many of the children will continue to see each other, they still need to engage in termination with this particular group. Members evaluate their experiences, talk about what each person has contributed to the group, examine what they've learned about problem solving, consider how they can transfer their learning to situations outside of the group, and think about how they can build on what they have learned. Review and reinforcement are key components of leader activities at this stage.

Complexities and Challenges Of Group Development

Although we have presented group development in an ordered, sequential manner, remember that group development is not always linear. Groups sometimes skip stages or move back to earlier stages, or features of early stages of development may reappear in later phases.

It may help to think of each single group session as moving through the phases of development, from planning, to forming, to storming, to performing, to termination. Each time members get together they must make connections anew, join the group in process, and focus on the work of that session. In the *Making Choices* groups, the goals of each session vary with the lesson of the day, and students must understand these specific goals and engage in activities designed to promote their achievement.

Group leaders can influence the course of group development by the actions they take. Leaders help children build supportive relationships, problem solve together, and enforce group rules. Leaders affect group process by implementing activities that encourage positive relationships and promote goal achievement. They monitor group

conflict and draw reticent or resistant members into the group interactions. They encourage group members to perform leadership functions themselves, as members contribute to the accomplishment of group objectives and strengthen peer relationships. As a group leader, you will want to ensure that your group develops its maximum potential for implementing *Making Choices* so that members can derive maximum benefit from the experience.

Guidelines for Making Choices Groups

Below are several guidelines for facilitating the development of *Making Choices* groups. The list is not exhaustive, and not every guideline will be applicable for all groups. However, in general, following these guidelines should enable you to optimize the group experience and help students master problem-solving skills.

- Use go-arounds to get all members involved at the beginning of each session.
- Call on more reticent members— make sure that all group members are included.
- Engage more positive and prosocial children in promoting the goals and activities of the group.
- Foster positive interactions among members.
- Help more aggressive or less-skilled students carry out prosocial activities in the group.

- Have clear rules (examples appear in the "Getting Started" section). In particular, have rules against put-downs, laughing at each other, and physical aggression.
- Get members involved in making and enforcing rules. Repeat rules frequently. Post or display them.
- Make sure members know the goals for the group and for themselves. Repeat—frequently—the goals of the sessions and of the group.
- Make sure members know their responsibilities to contribute to the group and to help each other. Encourage sharing and mutual aid throughout the life of the group.
- Stay in control of the process; intervene whenever and as often as needed. Don't prolong the storming phase.
- Use instances of conflict to demonstrate and reinforce the *Making Choices* content.
- Consider member characteristics and current interactions when you divide children into subgroups for activities.
- Plan activities and subgrouping so that each person can succeed and can be accepted.
- Help children to get out of roles after a role play—debrief group members, so that hostile emotions or negative behaviors are not carried beyond the role play.
- Remember that each group session goes through phases of group development, and you need to plan for that session, engage members, and terminate.

In several of the lessons you will find reminders about these guidelines, as well as additional information on how to deal with issues that are likely to come up because of the particular content or type of activity included in that lesson.

Making the Group A Positive Experience

Finally, we hope group leaders and students will *enjoy* taking part in *Making Choices* groups. We suggest that you take five or 10 minutes at the end of each session for a fun activity or snack. Group leaders should look for ways to make this a positive experience for each student. As we emphasize in the first session, catch the children being good and praise them when you do so. Encourage a warm, accepting atmosphere whenever the group meets. The children will be more receptive to the concepts and skills presented, and they will be more likely to want to come back.

Note: We have attempted to keep the language of this curriculum gender-neutral. At times we do this by using terms such as "he and she", especially in simple examples and short statements. With more complex examples, this usage becomes awkward and, instead, we use gender-specific language, alternating between masculine and feminine examples. Please note also that "children" are also referred to as "students" and "members" throughout the curriculum.

GETTING STARTED

OBJECTIVE

During this session, the students and group leaders will meet and get to know one another. Students will learn more about the purpose of the group and about group rules and expectations. Finally, students will become familiar with the group's system of behavioral incentives.

ACTIVITIES

Introductions. Have each person (group leaders included) give his or her name along with a brief descriptive statement. Children can give their ages and grades and information about something personal (but not embarrassing), such as their favorite subjects in school or their favorite TV shows. Keep introductions brief. Once everyone has spoken, the group leaders should lead the students in an icebreaker exercise. For example, after having students in the group say their names, go around again and have each student say the name of the people on his or her right and left.

Materials

- Poster board and markers or crayons
- Flip chart or blackboard

Purpose of the group. Review the purpose of the group. Introduce the main concepts that will guide the group activities and lessons in upcoming sessions. Use language appropriate to the developmental level of the children.

Your purpose statement might begin with a general expression of the need for everyone to get along. It should also contain an age-appropriate statement that deals specifically with the content of *Making Choices*. Examples of purpose statements follow, together with the approximate ages for which the phrasing might be appropriate.

The purpose of this group is to help us get along with other kids and with adults and to help us set and reach our goals. During the group we will learn:

- *to listen and use words, not our hands, when we have a problem or when somebody is mean* (kindergarten)
- *to stop, look, listen, and think before we act, so that nobody gets hurt and so that nobody gets into trouble* (second grade)
- *to learn to stop and think, to look for clues that tell us what's going on, to think about what we really want from others, and about all the things we could do, before we act, so that everybody can get along better* (fourth through sixth grade).

Leaders should encourage the students to think about and actively discuss the group's purpose by asking specific questions, such as "Why is it important to be able to get along?" Have students

Group Process Tip: Begin to build the group. Provide opportunities for each member to share something about himself or herself and to get to know each of the other members. Help students to understand the group's purpose, and engage them in developing rules for the group.

work together to create a poster or banner stating the purpose of the group, with illustrations, for display during subsequent group sessions. Figure 4 (see Appendix), the "staircase poster," is an example of how to visually present the steps in solving social problems. Group leaders can use this poster or modify it to introduce this material to students.

Rules and Expectations. Rules are expectations for behavior. They help the group run smoothly. Students should be invited to contribute rules they think are important. We suggest that group leaders ensure that the following five ground rules are included:[1]

- *Treat others as we would like to be treated. This includes no name calling, teasing, hitting, or threatening.*
- *Listen to each other, and wait for others to finish talking before we begin to speak.*
- *Keep control of our bodies and keep our hands to ourselves.*
- *What a person says in the group stays in the group.*
- *Everyone must participate in the activities of the group!*

Group leaders should feel free to rephrase these rules to suit their own teaching styles and the ages and cognitive levels of the children. (If rephrased, the rules should still be specific and behaviorally defined. Young children have difficulty understanding vague rules such as "be respectful.") Before revealing the above rules, it is a good idea to ask the children for suggestions to find out whether they come up with any of the five ground rules on their own. Having children actively take part in setting the rules helps them feel like they belong in the group, and it may increase their sense of power and control.

Once the rules have been agreed upon, they should be posted prominently in the room. A possible activity for the introductory session is to have children create a poster listing group rules, with each child drawing a picture depicting a student following a rule. Group leaders should refer to the rules and expectations frequently, so that everyone learns them by heart.

Incentives and Consequences. To help the group run smoothly and be productive, a system of incentives (rewards) and consequences should be used in conjunction with the group rules. One way to do this is to give children five chips or tokens at the beginning of each group meeting. Allow them to earn additional tokens by active participation in the group, by setting a good example, or by following group rules. Group leaders should be generous with rewards, allowing children to earn

---

[1] Depending on the makeup of the group, group leaders may wish to cover this material immediately after the introductions, before dealing with the purpose of the group.

23

as many chips as possible. For example, group leaders can always be on the lookout for desirable behavior and reward the child with a token, while matter-of-factly naming the "good deed" performed: for example, "Alissa, I really liked the way you let Thomas finish speaking before you said anything. You deserve a token." This draws the attention of the other group members to the positive behavior as well as to the reward that Alissa received for performing it.

Children can also lose tokens because of their behavior. Imposing this consequence should not be arbitrary, and group leaders should refer to a specific rule when taking tokens. The best strategy for maintaining group order and productivity is for group leaders to be alert for early warning signals that a child is having difficulty following a rule. When this happens, group leaders may wish to respond using a "reminder-warning-consequence" For example, "Alan, I see you're having a problem with Sarah. I'm giving you a reminder that the rule says you need to keep your hands to yourself." If the behavior persists, the group leader gives a warning, such as, "Alan, this is a *warning* that you need to keep your

hands to yourself, or you will lose one of your chips." And, if the behavior continues to persist, the group leader implements the consequence with a simple statement such as, "I'm really sorry, but I need to take one of your chips. Here's how you can earn it back."

Group leaders should implement this sequence in a neutral and low-key manner and always end with a reminder of how the child can earn back the lost chip. Of course, in the case of a sudden or serious outburst, this sequence may be impossible, and group leaders should have a plan ready for how to deal with such a situation. It may also be a good idea to include a statement about the reminder-warning-consequence sequence on the poster showing the rules of the group.[2]

Group leaders should provide a variety of items that can be purchased with the tokens. Be sure to have a wide range of age-appropriate items available that will appeal to a variety of students. Stickers and pencils may cost 5 tokens, a box of crayons may cost 25, and a stuffed animal may cost 50. When working with older students, group leaders may want to encourage students to pool their tokens and work toward group-focused

---

[2] Group leaders should use their judgment in determining how difficult or easy it might be for students to earn back a lost chip. In early phases it might be relatively more easy to earn back chips than in later phases, when students can be expected to have incorporated more group norms and to have developed skills in emotional regulation.

prizes—such as a trip to a favorite restaurant. Students should have the opportunity to cash in their tokens at the end of each meeting, so be sure to provide ample time for that activity. Many students will want to save their tokens, in which case group leaders may want to have students design special boxes or envelopes where students can store the tokens they have earned.

Anticipating the Next Session.

Encourage students to think about the purpose of the group and its rules. One way to do this is to have students think up possible names for the group that would reflect its purpose. You could begin the next session by soliciting ideas about names for the group.

UNIT 1: LEARNING ABOUT EMOTIONS AND FEELINGS

The emotional state of a child during a social situation plays an important role in how the problem-solving sequence is completed. The immediate feelings that a child is experiencing, the affect he or she displays, as well as more enduring characteristics, such as the child's skill in recognizing his or her own and others' feelings or, in some cases, mood disorders, can influence the steps of the problem-solving sequence (Branden-Muller, Elias, Gara, & Schneider, 1992; Graham et al., 1992; Quiggle, Garber, Panak, & Dodge, 1992).

The goal of this unit is to increase each child's ability to identify basic emotions and to increase awareness of how people experience feelings in different ways. Children will also become familiar with simple strategies, such as self-talk, to identify and manage their own feelings.

Children who are extremely angry, upset, or sad, for example, are likely to have difficulty encoding and interpreting cues accurately, in formulating goals and responses that are oriented towards positive relationships, and in selecting and enacting appropriate responses (Crick & Dodge, 1994). In other words, when children are experiencing a high level of emotion in a social situation, they are less likely to be able to stop and think before they act. Before they can learn and use the skills presented in this curriculum, children must be able to recognize how they and others are feeling during a situation. Recognizing feelings is the first step in learning how to stop and think.

Lesson 1: Recognizing and Identifying Feelings

OBJECTIVE

Children will be able to identify, describe, and label eight feelings: (1) happy, (2) sad, (3) angry (upset, mad), (4) satisfied (OK), (5) nervous, (6) relaxed, (7) frightened (scared), and (8) safe. For younger children, concentrate on two, three, or four basic feelings—perhaps happy, mad, and sad. Introduce additional feelings only if children appear to have mastered the basic feelings.

Materials

- "Feeling face cards" (grades K-3) illustrating the eight feelings (Make enough copies of the cards so that each student gets two cards; see activity sheets 1 to 2)
- Pictures from magazines showing children and adolescents expressing the eight emotions (grades 4-6)
- A list of five to 10 fill-in-the-blank "feeling statements" to be read aloud (see number 4 below)

REVIEW

Going around the group, ask each child to identify one of the ground rules developed during the introductory session. Ask for a volunteer to explain the system of tokens, that is, how they can be earned and what they can be used for. Review the reminder-warning-consequence sequence, relating it to the group's rules. If you wish to come up with a name for the group, solicit students' ideas during the review. Write down a short list of appropriate suggestions and tell the students the group will decide on a name during the next session.

ACTIVITIES

1. Discuss with the children the idea that people have many different feelings and many different ways of expressing their feelings. People can use words to describe how they feel, but they can also express feelings with their bodies, for example, with their faces. Mention each of the eight feelings, then ask the students to try making a happy face, a sad face, a frightened face, a nervous face, and so on.

2. Give each student two feeling face cards (or pictures). Ask the children to identify the feelings on their cards and to describe what the face is doing (frowning, smiling, and so on). Then ask students to talk about a situation that might make them feel this way. Provide examples as needed.

3. After all of the students have described their face cards, ask them, one at a time, to walk around the room and match their cards with the opposite feeling face card. With young children, and as needed with older children, ask each to practice saying: "The opposite of [frowning, for example] is [smiling, for example]." Very young children may have problems understanding opposites. If

Group Process Tip: Use go-arounds to get all members involved at the beginning of the session. Engage more positive and prosocial group members in defining initial goals and activities. Draw all members into the activities and interactions.

students are having difficulty, concentrate on basic pairs such as happy/sad, mad/glad, and so on.

4. Finally, read aloud the list of prepared feeling statements. Initially, the group leader should read the entire statement, including the blanks to be filled in by the students: for example, "I feel [happy] when I play with my best friend, not [sad]." Repeating the statement, the group leader will pause and allow the children to call out an appropriate response. The group leader may call on a student individually, or allow the group to answer together. The statements could look like this:

- I feel *happy* when I play with my best friend, not *sad*.
- Heather feels *angry* when her mom yells at her, not *satisfied*.
- The boy felt *frightened* when he was lost, not *safe*.

Be sure to phrase the statements in an age-appropriate way. (For a sixth-grader, for example, you might phrase the first statement like this: "I feel happy when I get to ride my bike over to my friend's house, not sad.") It is important to keep in mind that children's responses may vary. Group leaders should allow for this and be aware that a response is not necessarily right or wrong.

SUMMARIZE THE MAIN IDEA

Ask for a volunteer to summarize the main points discussed today: (1) People can have many different feelings, and (2) they express their feelings with words and in other ways (for example, with their faces). If needed, the group leader can restate the main points and ask students to give examples both with words and with their faces.

Note: Each lesson concludes with a restatement of the main idea, as indicated above. In subsequent lessons we simply state the idea in italics, without instructions to group leaders. We encourage group leaders to use the review section to have students summarize, and (for older children) give their own views on, the main ideas covered. To ensure broad participation, group leaders may alternate asking for volunteers and calling on students to summarize main points.

LESSON ENRICHMENT ACTIVITY

Have students make a feelings collage of facial expressions by cutting faces out of magazines. Children must identify the feeling on the faces they cut out before adding them to the collage.

ACTIVITY SHEET 1: FEELING FACE CARDS

SAD

When I feel like

CRY

SORRY

Things are going badly for me or I lost something or somebody.

UNHAPPY

SAFE

When I feel like

SECURE

PROTECTED

I can take care of myself or someone is watching over me.

ALL RIGHT

FRIGHTENED

When I feel like

WORRIED

AFRAID

Something bad might happen or I don't have control of things.

SCARED

SATISFIED

When I feel like

PEACEFUL

CONTENTED

Things are fair or everything is OK.

FULFILLED

ACTIVITY SHEET 2: FEELING FACE CARDS

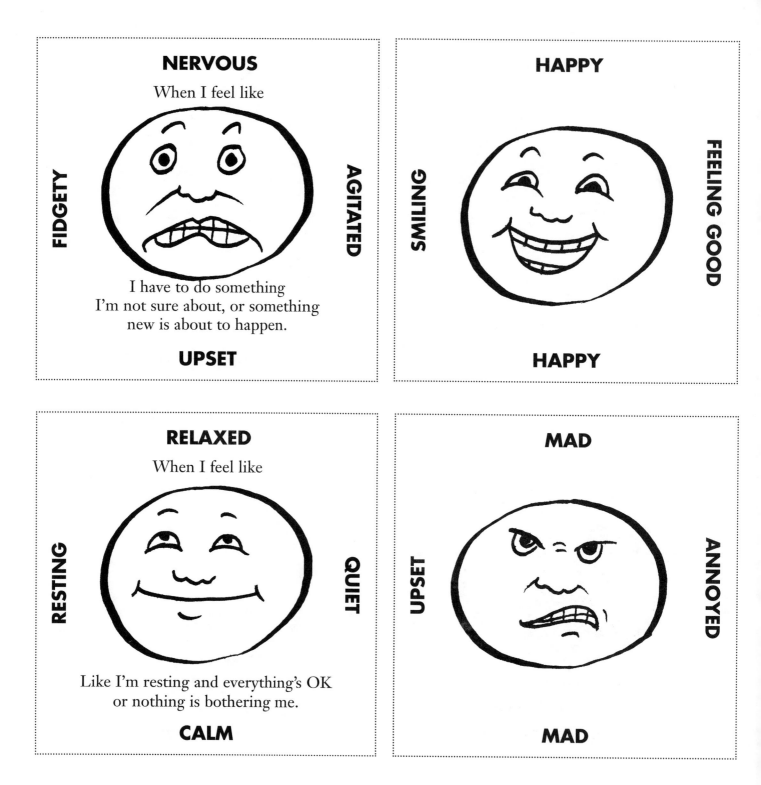

NERVOUS

When I feel like

FIDGETY

AGITATED

I have to do something
I'm not sure about, or something
new is about to happen.

UPSET

HAPPY

SMILING

FEELING GOOD

HAPPY

RELAXED

When I feel like

RESTING

QUIET

Like I'm resting and everything's OK
or nothing is bothering me.

CALM

MAD

UPSET

ANNOYED

MAD

30

Lesson 2: Matching Feelings with Situations

OBJECTIVE

Children will be able to match selected feelings with specific situations and social contexts. This lesson should also improve children's listening skills.

Materials

- "Feeling bingo cards" (see activity sheet 3)
- Chips (or any type of marker for children to mark their bingo cards)
- A list of about 50 age-appropriate situations, each related to one of the feelings you have covered
- Stickers or some other small token to award to winners

REVIEW

Ask students to recall the feelings they talked about in lesson 1. Ask them to describe situations when they might feel a certain way.

ACTIVITIES

1. Pass out one feeling bingo card and several chips to each student. Ask students to fill in the blank squares with the feelings you have been discussing. Depending on the number of feelings you've covered, students may need to write down one or more feelings more than once. They can fill them in wherever they want. Point out that each of the cards has a "free" space in the center. (Group leaders should fill out cards beforehand for younger children.)

2. Explain to the students that you will be reading aloud to the class about certain situations. After a statement has been read, students should mark their bingo cards according to the emotion that they believe corresponds to the situation. Once a child has filled in her or his card with three chips in a row across, down, or diagonally, she or he should call out "Bingo."

3. A child who gets bingo should name the feelings that are marked and, if able, identify the situation that prompted the answer. Assist children as needed in recalling the situations, soliciting help from the others. Finally, ask the winner if he or she can give an example of other words that describe these feelings.

4. The game should be played several times, until all situations are exhausted. Ask several students to think about something that makes them happy (sad, angry, and so on). Then play the game again and ask students whether their feelings affected how they heard the clues.

Keep your list of situations simple—limit them to one or two sentences. Keep each statement focused on only one emotion, but remember that some children may choose a feeling different from the one intended. The goal is to have children explain why they selected a particular feeling. Prompt students to discuss other feelings that may have been appropriate.

Group Process Tip: The game in this lesson is designed to promote discussion about linking feelings with specific contexts. Remember to model for students how to respond to others' comments and to encourage their participation in the discussion. Try to recognize a contribution by each student, no matter how minor, in order to help students feel like they are valued group members. Reinforce students' positive responses or comments to one another.

Examples are provided below. You may want older students to generate their own list of situations. If so, have them break down into small groups to generate a list of three or four situations each. After each situation, ask, "How would you feel?" or "How would the person feel?"

EXAMPLES OF SITUATIONS FOR BINGO

- You are on the playground and run up to a girl who is on the only swing. She sees you and calls out, "Do you want to use the swing? I can take turns with you."

- One day at the pool you are practicing holding your head under water. Suddenly a big kid puts his hand on your head and holds it there for a few seconds. When you pull away from him, he jumps out of the pool and laughs at you.

- After school, you go with some other kids to play softball, but you have to stop at your house on the way. You ask your friend to save you a good glove, but when you get to the field, your friend says there isn't a good glove for you.

- You are working on your spelling at home one night. When you have just finished the last problem, your sister comes into the room, carrying a glass of milk and a big book. She starts to ask you about a picture in the book when the glass of milk spills out of her hand. The milk runs all over your spelling and ruins it.

- At school one day you are trying to read a book that is pretty hard. A kid in your class comes over and can tell that the book is hard for you. The kid says in a loud voice that he read that book last year and it was easy and that you must be a pretty bad reader if it's hard for you.

- When you are eating in the cafeteria, you see a bunch of kids talking and laughing on the other side of the room. One of them looks over at your table and says something to the others. The other kids laugh even louder.

- There are two boys using the Legos when you come into the classroom one morning. You ask them if you can play, too. The boys don't say anything so you ask them again. One of the boys looks up at you and says that they don't want you to play because you smell funny.

- When you are playing with blocks at school one day, you cannot find the big green blocks that make neat towers. A girl comes and asks if she can help you find the big green blocks.

- You are walking home from school one day when you come to the apartment of your best friend. There are several kids from your class playing with your friend in the front, and it looks like they're having fun. You had talked with your friend earlier, but she didn't ask you to come over.

- During a relay race, you are running very fast and are in first place. When you try to hand over the baton to the next kid on your team, the kid drops the baton and you both fall on the ground.

- You are working hard on your arithmetic homework one night, but just can't seem to get one problem right. Your older brother comes into the room and looks at your homework. He says he would be glad to help you with the problem if you want him to.

- One day you are walking to school wearing a new pair of basketball shoes that you've been wanting to get for weeks. As you are about to go onto the school grounds, a kid runs into you, making you step right into a big mud puddle. The kid looks at you, says he is sorry, and asks you if you are okay.

- At lunchtime you walk into the cafeteria with your friend and you see that there is only one cheeseburger left. You tell your friend how much you like cheeseburgers. Your teacher stops you and asks you a question before you can get in line. When you get in line, you see that the last cheeseburger is on your friend's tray.

- One day you are swimming at the pool where you always go, but you don't see any of your friends. It's starting to get really boring and you wish you had somebody to play with. Just then a kid comes over and tells you he is bored. He asks you if you want to practice low dives.

- After lunch one day you are talking with a group of friends. A boy from your class comes up and joins the group. He interrupts you and tells the others that they shouldn't listen to what you are saying because you never know what you're talking about.

- You can't wait to show your mom the good grade you got on your science project. You are waiting for her to pick you up and your project is sitting right beside you on the sidewalk.

- While you're waiting, you see two kids riding their bikes on the sidewalk, and they are laughing and not watching where they are going.

- You call out to them and they look at you and try to put on their brakes real fast, but it's too late and one of the kids runs over your science project, smashing it.

LESSON ENRICHMENT ACTIVITY

Read *How Do I Feel?*, by Norma Simon, a story about identifying feelings. It encourages children to suggest how the main character might feel as he encounters a variety of situations.

ACTIVITY SHEET 3: FEELING BINGO

Lesson 3: Identifying Physical Responses to Feelings

OBJECTIVE

Students will be able to identify how their bodies may respond to each of the feelings discussed in lesson 1: happy, sad, angry, satisfied, nervous, relaxed, frightened, and safe.

Materials

- Illustrated outline of a child's body labeled with a feeling (one sheet for each child) (See activity sheets 4 to 7 for four basic feelings; leaders can modify these sheets to include additional feelings as needed.)
- Markers, crayons, or colored pencils

REVIEW

Review by asking students to recall the eight feelings introduced in lesson 1. Talk about how these feelings might vary according to the situation or context—for example, on the playground (with adult supervision) versus on the street (without adult supervision). This can be accomplished by going around the group and asking each student to name one or two feelings and situations in which they might occur. During the review you can also go over the list of suggested names for the group and help the students decide which one they prefer. If a name is chosen, students may wish to spend the last five minutes of the session working on a logo or symbol depicting the group and its name.

ACTIVITIES

1. Explain to the children that they will receive a worksheet with an outline of a person's body. Each worksheet is labeled with a feeling. Using this sheet, children should draw in a face that corresponds to the labeled feeling.

2. Once the children have completed the faces, they should mark with X's the places on the body where they might feel this emotion. Group leaders should post an example of this, and explain to students why they marked the body where they did. Here are some examples:

- *Angry:* I get a tight, "scrunched-up" feeling in my face; My leg starts to shake and my foot jumps up and down.
- *Sad:* My eyes start to fill with tears.
- *Happy:* My whole body starts to move; my voice gets very loud.
- *Frightened:* I get a dizzy feeling in my stomach; I get "hyper" all over.

Group Process Tip: As children discuss feelings, be sure to pay attention to—and stay in control of—the group process. For example, don't let students dwell on negative feelings at the expense of positive feelings. Help members to become supportive of each other's efforts.

3. Depending on the ages of the children, group leaders should be prepared for some silly and even sexually oriented examples from the students. The former can be ignored for the most part. As for the latter, the group leader should listen to determine whether the student is just being silly, in which case redirecting the discussion is called for (for example, "Let's just talk about parts of your body

like your head, your stomach, or your arms and legs"). If a student seems to be expressing a genuine concern (or if you are in doubt), offer to talk about the issue later with the child, apart from the group, perhaps with a guidance counselor or school social worker.

4. Have each student describe his or her picture. Be sure to ask each student what the face is doing and how the person is feeling. The students can also be asked to demonstrate the emotion on the face they drew. Ask each child to explain how this emotion might feel in his or her body. Group leaders should provide language and examples as needed.

5. After all of the pictures have been described, ask each student, one at a time, to walk around the room and find the opposite feeling. Group leaders should then briefly describe the differences between the pairs of pictures. A way to phrase this might be, "Happiness looks like this, while sadness looks look this." Also, group leaders might wish to hold up a drawing while asking students to show with their faces what the feeling looks like and with their bodies where they might feel it.

SUMMARIZE THE MAIN IDEA

Many times, different parts of our bodies let us know how we are feeling. We can feel emotions in our face, hands, legs, and other parts of our body.

LESSON ENRICHMENT ACTIVITY

For children in kindergarten through third grade, read the story *Nelson Makes a Face*, by Burton Cohen. This is a story of how a fairy godmother tries to teach a lesson to a prankster named Nelson by freezing his face with three different emotions: sadness, happiness, and anger.

ACTIVITY SHEET 4: FEELING FACES

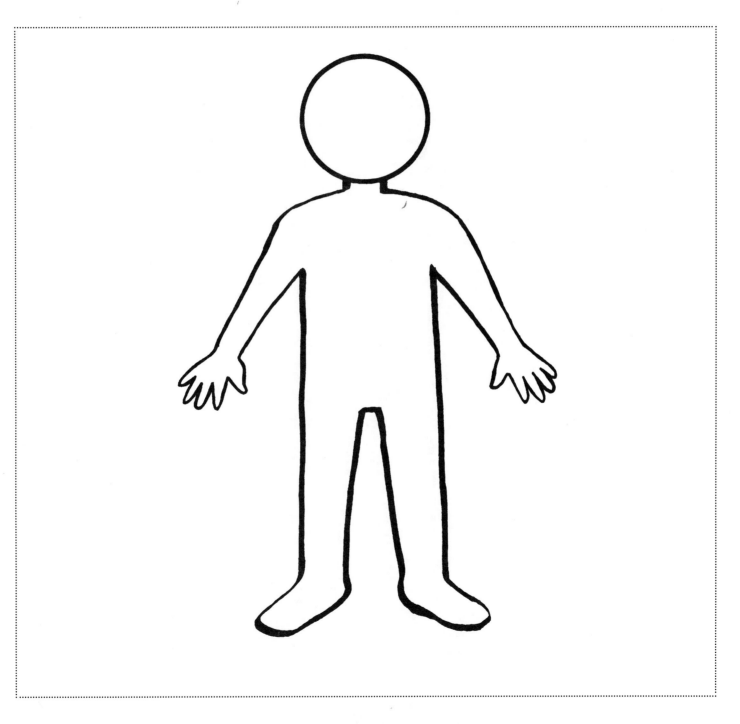

HAPPY

ACTIVITY SHEET 5: FEELING FACES

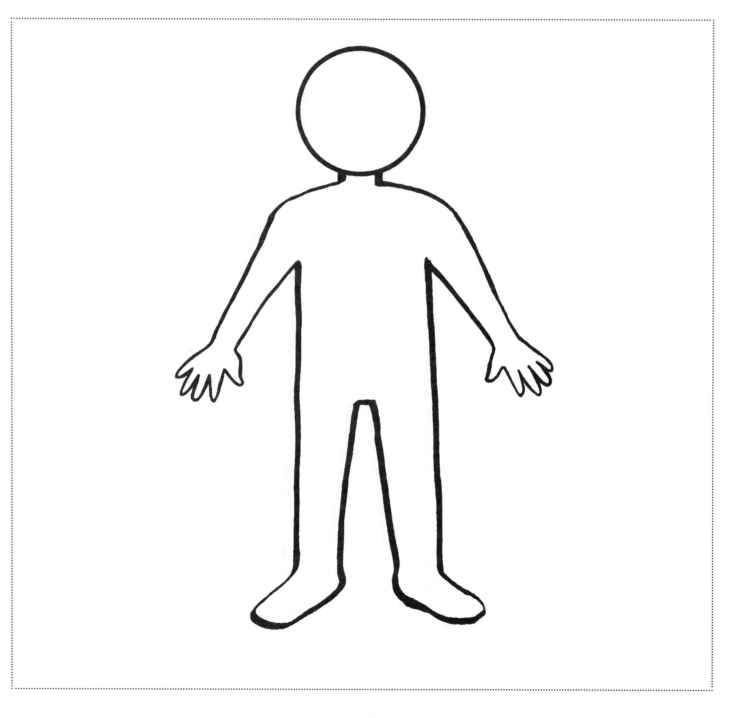

ANGRY

ACTIVITY SHEET 6: FEELING FACES

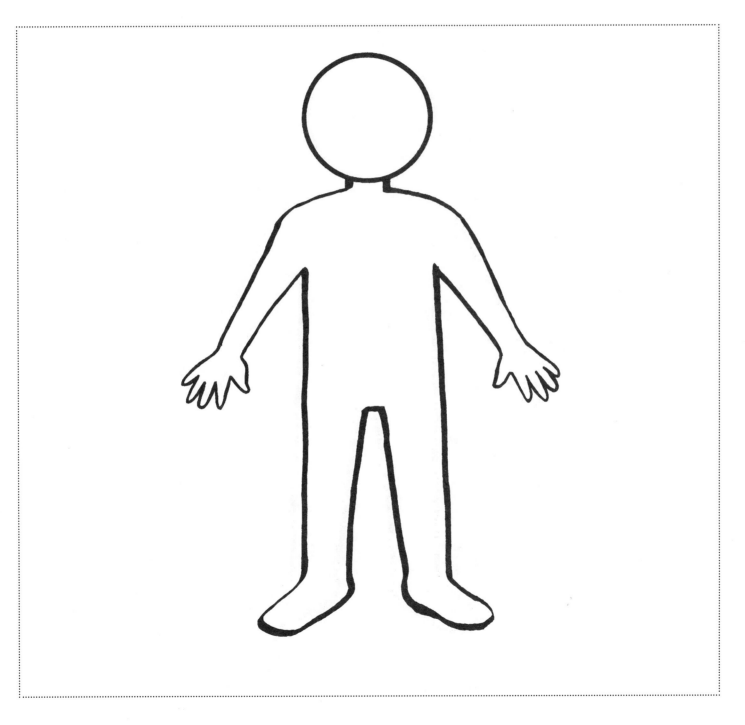

SAD

ACTIVITY SHEET 7: FEELING FACES

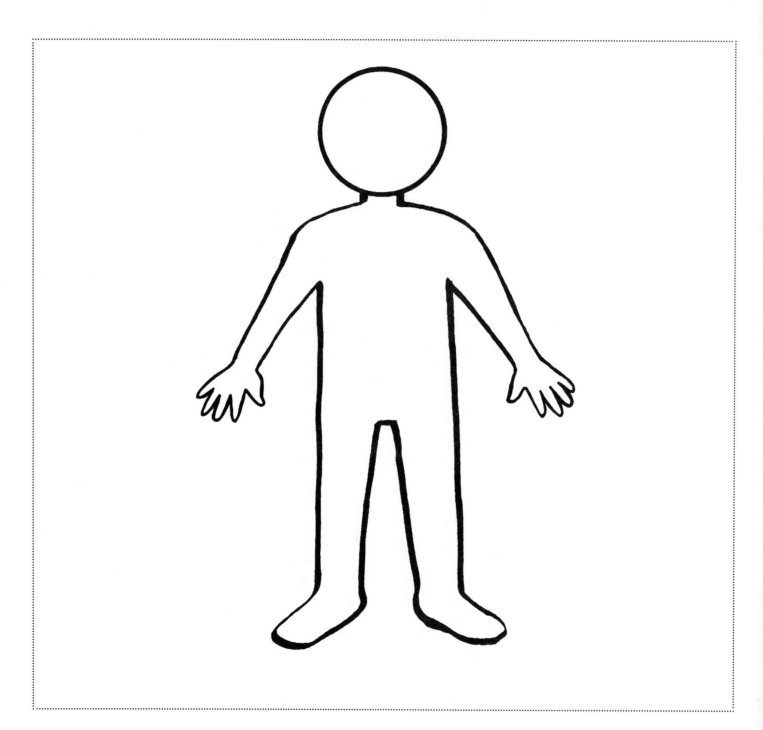

FRIGHTENED

Lesson 4: Degrees of Feelings—Anger

OBJECTIVE

Children will be able to describe how people may experience different degrees of a feeling in different situations. Focusing on anger, children will be able to state the difference between mild anger ("a little bit angry") and severe anger ("really angry").

Materials

- Activity sheets 8 to 10 and crayons or markers
- Flip chart or blackboard
- Tape or pushpins to post the activity sheets

REVIEW

Review the feelings discussed in the previous sessions. Ask students to take turns making a statement associated with a specific feeling (for example, "I'm really happy when I get a good report from my teacher!"). Instruct each student to use his or her body and voice to express the feeling. Ask others to describe what they see and hear.

ACTIVITIES

1. Explain that today's activities will focus on anger. Ask students to think of a time when they felt angry. Going around the group, have them describe what happened, how they felt, and how they responded. Prompt students to label the anger on a "feeling thermometer" of low to high. Group leaders can provide examples of other words to describe the degree of anger (really mad, kind of angry, medium, and so on).

2. Pass out activity sheets 8 to 10 to each student. Ask students to draw a picture that corresponds to the level of anger stated on their worksheet. (You can easily modify these sheets by changing feeling "angry" to feeling "mad" or, for very young children, feeling "bad.")

3. After the pictures are completed, post them on the wall in groups corresponding to degrees of anger.

4. Have each student describe his or her drawing. Encourage students to specify what's happening in the picture, how it might feel, and how these feelings could come out through facial expressions and body language.

5. Group leaders should chart responses on a flip chart or blackboard and summarize how different situations led to different degrees of anger, which, in turn, brought about different bodily responses. A chart might look like this:

Group Process Tip: This lesson is about anger. Stay in control of the process so that activities focus on the discussion of anger without devolving into re-enacting anger. The lesson is not designed to be cathartic or emotive. Rather, we want children to learn about levels of anger. Encourage members to ask questions and participate. Because this is a potentially difficult topic, leave a little more time than usual at the end of the session to have a special snack or play a favorite game.

41

Situation	Degree of Anger	How it looked and felt
Sue teased me.	low	I frowned and I felt a lump in my throat.
My brother hit me.	high	My face turned red, my heart pounded, I cried.

SUMMARIZE THE MAIN IDEA

We can feel very angry about one thing, while a different thing might make us just a little bit angry.

LESSON ENRICHMENT ACTIVITY

Have students brainstorm situations that make them angry. Have pairs of students role play or puppet play the situations; be sure to point out the degree of anger produced by the incident and the body cues revealed. End by asking students to identify things that help them feel better after getting angry. Ask if anyone ever decided not to get angry. Be sure to debrief students after the role play—that is, help them leave the role play (and their anger) behind.

ACTIVITY SHEET 8

I Feel Mildly Angry When...

ACTIVITY SHEET 8A

I Feel A Little Bit Angry When...

ACTIVITY SHEET 9

I Feel Moderately Angry When...

ACTIVITY SHEET 9A

I Feel Pretty Angry When...

ACTIVITY SHEET 10

I Feel Very Angry When...

ACTIVITY SHEET 10A

I Feel Extremely Angry When...

Lesson 5: Recognizing and Managing Feelings

OBJECTIVE

Students will be able to identify several basic steps that can be used to recognize and manage their own feelings.

REVIEW

Materials

■ Copy of *The Turtle Story!* and pictures of turtles or stuffed toy turtles

Ask students to name the feelings discussed in this unit and to explain different ways people experience them. Review the idea that people experience different degrees of feelings. Name a few common classroom and after-school situations, and ask children to identify a feeling the situation might bring up, as well as how strong this feeling would be.

ACTIVITIES

1. Explain that you will be reading a story written especially to help children learn to recognize and manage anger, frustration, sadness, and other difficult feelings. For younger students, you might explain that they are going to learn how to know their feelings and how to calm down. Discuss the importance of learning how to manage these feelings. Explain that sometimes, when we can't manage difficult feelings, we act out of control and cause more problems for ourselves. (Provide examples as needed, such as "I got so mad I ran off and missed the ball game.")

2. Before you begin reading the story, ask young children if they know what a turtle is. Distribute pictures and toys and ask students to describe the features of turtles. Ask students what they think the shell is for. Praise students for their ideas, and encourage them to listen carefully so that they can find out a secret use of a turtle's shell.

3. Read the turtle story aloud, or paraphrase it. For older children, read the story and ask them to develop two skits, one that shows and one that does not show use of the turtle technique. Each skit might have a narrator who summarizes the moral of the story.

4. Ask these follow-up questions: Did you like the turtle story? Why or why not? Do you ever feel like Ralph or Lesley? Explain.

Give examples of times when you could use the turtle secret.

Review the four steps of the turtle's secret: (1) recognize (or acknowledge), (2) relax, (3) think, (4) do. Practice the four steps with hypothetical situations.

Encourage students to think of alternative ways they can "go into their

Group Process Tip: Group leaders should make it a point to model self-talk steps for students during this lesson. Provide examples for which self-talk has helped you in a difficult situation. Elicit from group members their own ideas of what they might say to themselves. Continue to help members build a system of mutual aid.

49

shells"—close their eyes, go to time out, put their heads down, walk away from conflict, and so on.

5. Develop two or three turtle-like stories with the students, based on possible or actual conflict situations. These scripts should be very basic. For example,

Anthony sees Paul with a magic marker just like the one he lost yesterday, so when Paul isn't looking, Anthony takes it . . . but Paul catches him.

6. Using puppets, students should act out each scene, freezing the skit at the point of conflict. Solicit input from the students in the audience, encouraging them to use the turtle's secret to help frame their solutions. Then have the puppets act out the suggested solutions.

7. After each skit, ask students the following questions:
- How do you think the puppets were feeling?
- Do you think they were saying anything to themselves to keep from losing control?
- What kinds of things were they saying?

8. Explain to students that they will have many more opportunities to learn about and practice ideas described in the story. Emphasize that right now, they are learning about feelings, and how to recognize different feelings. As they continue in the *Making Choices* program they will learn more about how to think about the situations they are in, what they might do, and how to choose the best thing to do.

SUMMARIZE THE MAIN IDEA

Sometimes when we are getting into a problem, we're not sure how we feel. It can be helpful to stop and think and to talk to ourselves about how we might be feeling.

LESSON ENRICHMENT ACTIVITY

Have students create shells of their own by coloring a turtle shell on a paper grocery bag. Have students recall and then write down on the bag the four steps of the turtle's secret. Students can slip into their shell when they need to relax or use it to remember the four steps.

THE TURTLE STORY![1]

Once upon a time there was a handsome young turtle. He was nine years old, and he had just started the fourth grade.[2] His name was Ralph. Ralph was very upset about going to school. He didn't want to learn school things. He wanted to run

---

[1] Adapted from Marlene Schneider & Arthur Robin, Point Woods Laboratory, Stony Brook, New York, 11794.

[2] Use the age and grade that fit your audience.

outside or stay at home to watch television. It was too hard to try to write letters and learn about numbers. It didn't seem fair to him that he should have to do so much work. He would rather play and laugh with friends.

Ralph got into lots of fights with other turtles, but he really didn't know how they started. He felt he had to fight. He didn't like listening to his teacher or having to stop making those wonderful loud fire engine noises he used to make with his mouth. It was too hard to be good in school. It seemed as though he was mad or unhappy most of the time and always in trouble.

Every day on his way to school Ralph would say to himself that he would try his best not to get into trouble that day. But despite his plans, every day he would get mad at somebody and fight, or he would get angry because he made a mistake, and then he would rip up his papers. He always got into trouble—he just hated school! He began to feel like a "bad" turtle. He went around for a long time feeling very, very bad.

There was also another turtle in his class named Lesley. She lived close to Ralph and sometimes they walked home from school together. She was a nice young turtle, but she didn't like school either. In fact she didn't like much of anything. She felt sad or worried most of the time.

Lesley worried about her mother and father. She worried that her mother might get sick or that her father might lose his job. She worried because her parents sometimes argued. She worried that her teachers would get mad at her. She worried about everything. When she was worried, sometimes she was sad. She remembered that her cat got lost last year, and she missed her cat. She was sad about herself, too. She didn't like the way she looked. She didn't like her clothes. In fact, she didn't like much of anything.

She didn't do well in school either. She was so worried and sad that she never really got interested in doing her school work. She was always thinking about other things. She worried about her classmates, too. Sometimes she wanted to play with them and make friends, but she worried that they wouldn't like her or that they would call her stupid or ugly.

One day Ralph and Lesley were walking home from school together. They were both feeling very unhappy, when they met the biggest, oldest turtle in their town. The wise old turtle was 200 years old and as big as a house. Both Ralph and Lesley had heard stories about how the wise old turtle helped other turtles feel better about themselves. They had heard that the old turtle had lived in many lands, knew many things, and had seen floods and fires from years ago.

So Ralph told the old turtle that he was feeling bad. He told the old turtle about the fights, about the ripped-up papers, and about getting into trouble. Lesley told the old turtle about feeling sad and worried all the time. The young turtles were a little afraid, but they told the old turtle anyway.

The old tortoise smiled at them in a kindly way and seemed eager to help them. "My goodness," the tortoise said in a big bellowing voice. Then the old turtle's voice became soft and quiet. "I'll tell you a secret," he said. "You are carrying the answer to your problem around with you."

Ralph and Lesley didn't know what the old turtle was talking about. Still whispering, the old turtle said, "Your shell! Your shell! That's why you have a shell. You can go inside your shell when you feel sad or when you seem to be heading for trouble. When you are in your shell, you can have a moment to rest and think about things so you can figure out what to do next."

Lesley and Ralph still looked a bit puzzled. So the old turtle said, "Here's what you can do when you feel like you are troubled or heading for trouble. Ralph, say to yourself, 'I feel angry.' Lesley, say to yourself, 'I feel worried.' Then say to yourself, 'Go into my shell to relax.'"

In your shell you are safe. You can relax all the muscles of your body. You can let them get limp, like cooked spaghetti.

Then, for a few seconds, take a couple of deep breathes and blow your troubles out of your mouth, right out of your shell. Just rest for a moment."

Then say: 'I can think of a way to help myself.' Think of something you can do that might help you. Think of as many ideas as you can. Then think about the idea that has the best chance of helping you avoid trouble and helping you feel better."

Then come out of your shell and do it. Do the best thing you can do to help yourself."

Ralph and Lesley liked the idea, but they didn't understand it very well, so they asked the turtle to describe it again. The old turtle repeated what they should do. This time they practiced the steps as the old turtle told the story. The old turtle said, "When you feel troubled, remember the four parts of the 'Secret to a Happier Life':
- Say what you are feeling and recognize your feelings.
- Go into your shell and relax.
- Think of something you could do to help yourself.
- Then do it."

After they left the old turtle, Lesley started to worry. She started to wonder whether her mother and father would be in a good mood. But then she remembered what the old turtle had told her. She said, "I feel worried." Then she went into her shell to relax. After she rested for a moment, she began to think about ways she might help herself. At first, she began worrying again about her mother and father. Then she figured that worrying about them wouldn't do any good. While resting in her shell, she thought: "If they were in a bad mood, they would just be in a bad mood." She thought she could say she was sorry they felt bad and hoped they would feel better. She also thought she could try to take her mind off her parents, because she could not control how they felt. She thought about a new song she had heard on the radio. She decided to sing the new song. She liked the song and it helped her feel better. She felt proud that night with her new skill.

The next day, Lesley started to feel sad at school because she didn't like the way she looked. She remembered the four parts of the secret. She said to herself that she felt sad about the way she looked. Then she relaxed in her shell. At first, she thought of giving up, putting her head down and going to sleep. Then she thought of telling the teacher that she was sick so she could go home. But neither of those thoughts felt like they would really help her. Finally she figured out that she could look better if she washed the dirt off her shell during recess. She also figured out that she could be happier if she got her work done. She

did it and it helped again. Her secret helped her with a lot of her worried and sad feelings.

That evening, Ralph also thought about the special secret. He practiced saying its four parts: "Say what you feel, relax for a moment, think about helping yourself, and do something to help yourself." He said them over and over again. He told his parents about his secret and they seemed to like the idea. He was very eager to try out his new skill in school.

The next day came, and he again made a mistake on his nice clean paper. He started to feel that angry feeling again and was about to lose his temper, when suddenly he remembered what the old tortoise had said.

"I feel mad, but I don't need trouble," Ralph said to himself. Instead of ripping up his paper, he pulled in his arms, legs, and head and rested. At first he felt tense from his anger, but he took some deep breaths and blew his troubles out through his mouth. He was delighted to find how nice and comfortable it was in his shell. The mistake didn't bother him so much there. He thought about ways to deal with his angry feelings. He thought about throwing his pencil across the room, punching the girl in front of him, and ripping up his paper. None of those ideas seemed right. He figured out that the best thing to do was to go on with his work as best he could. When he came out of his shell, he felt better. As he continued working, he was surprised to find his teacher smiling at him. He told her he was angry about his mistake, but that he had decided to continue working. She said she was very proud of him!

Ralph and Lesley also used their secret to help make friends. Ralph noticed that he didn't hit people the way he used to. He used to punch, poke, or shove people all the time—and he usually got into trouble for it. Inside his shell, he found other things to do instead. Sometimes he would just say hello to other turtles, and at other times, when things didn't seem fair, he would tell them about things that bothered him. He felt like he didn't have to fight everyone anymore.

Lesley worried less about how her friends would treat her. Before the old turtle came, when people called her names like ugly or stupid, she just fell apart. Now she didn't. Instead, she would go inside her shell and give herself different messages, such as "I am a pretty turtle" or "making a mistake does not make me stupid." She felt stronger, and because she wasn't so worried about what other turtles might say or do to her, she could spend more time just playing around with them.

Both Ralph and Lesley continued using their secret for the rest of the year.

When they got angry, sad, or worried or felt themselves heading for trouble, they accepted their feelings, relaxed, thought for a while, and figured out what they could do to help themselves. Then they did it.

Lesley and Ralph didn't always make themselves feel better, and they didn't always know what to do, but they did do a lot better. They got into fewer fights and made more friends. They felt happier and got into less trouble. When they got their report cards, they got the best grades either of them had ever made. Everybody admired them and wondered what their magic secret was. Best of all, they felt proud of themselves.

Lesson 6: Practicing Self-Talk

OBJECTIVE

Students will be able to engage in simple self-talk in order to identify their feelings.

Materials

- Two large puppets and two finger puppets (grades K-3)
- Conflict situation cards

REVIEW

Review the four steps of the turtle secret. Remind students that one way to help us recognize (or acknowledge), relax, think, and do is to talk ourselves through it.

ACTIVITIES

1. Ask students to share a time when they have talked themselves through a difficult or challenging situation. Explain that this is self-talk which is an important ingredient in problem-solving. Continue to give examples of when self-talk has been helpful for you (for example, "I had to give a talk to a group of people and I was very nervous, so I kept telling myself I could do it").

2. Select two students to act out a conflict situation with the large puppets. Introduce two smaller finger puppets who will act as the self-talking puppets (or as the conscience of the larger puppets). Choose two more students to operate the finger puppets. The finger puppets can be compared to Jiminy Cricket—just as Jiminy Cricket helped Pinocchio solve problems, the self-talk puppets will help the larger puppets.

3. Choose a conflict situation and have the large puppets (students) act it out. Group leaders should freeze the scene several times, allowing the self-talk puppets (students) to take over and model self-talk statements. (Group leaders should review examples of self-talk and demonstrate the process one time.) Allow the children to make both positive and negative self-statements, prompting them to decide whether the self-talk is helping the puppets (students) label their feelings accurately or making them more angry (nervous, sad, scared, and so on).

Here are some examples of self-talk:

- "Josh is making fun of me and I am getting really angry! My face is red and my heart is pounding! I feel like I am going to lose control. I need to calm down."
- "The aide yelled at me for not cleaning up my area, but I did! I want to scream at her. That makes me so mad, and it hurts my feelings too. I really need to take a few deep breaths."
- "I have to sit next to Sharon on the

Group Process Tip: If you use role plays in this session, take care how members are paired so this will be a positive learning experience for them. Be sure to "debrief" students; that is, help them get out of the roles they took on during the role play. Make sure that group members reward each other and point out positive features of each others' self-talk.

bus! I never get to sit with anyone I like, and that's not fair. It makes me so mad! Maybe I should count to ten."

- "Billy got to use the computer before me! He got to go first yesterday, too! I never get to go first! I'm getting really mad here. I need to chill."
- "My little sister broke my necklace after I told her not to wear it. She is always in my stuff! She makes me really angry! I'm going to go in my room for ten minutes and calm down."
- "During recess, Maria tripped and I tried to help her but I fell down, too! Now my brand new pants are all dirty, and this afternoon we're having our class picture taken! I am so frustrated and disappointed! I'd better breathe in and out a couple of times."

4. When several scenes have been acted out, review the effects of self-talk with the students. Encourage students to consider the following questions:
- What things can you say to yourself to figure out how you're feeling?
- Does naming a feeling help you calm down, or not?
- How can you remember to use self-talk?
- Can your body's clues help you remember?

5. Explain to students that they are learning to use self-talk to recognize and relax during this lesson. Later they will learn about using it to think and do as well.

SUMMARIZE THE MAIN IDEA

We can often understand how we are feeling if we stop, think, and talk to ourselves about what is going on and how it makes us feel.

CONFLICT SITUATION CARDS

CONFLICT

Melanie and Kris are working on their homework together. Kris really wants to finish their math, but Melanie wants to chill.

CONFLICT

CONFLICT

Tom sees Paul wearing sneakers just like the ones that are missing from his locker. Her goes up to Paul and askes where he got the shoes.

CONFLICT

CONFLICT

Anthony is playing ball with his little brother in the park. A bunch of kids from his school go by and one of them yells something that sounds like a diss.

CONFLICT

CONFLICT

Anna's sister wants to call a friend but has been on the phone for an hour. Now Anna wants a turn, too, but her sister makes her call anyway.

CONFLICT

CONFLICT SITUATION CARDS

CONFLICT

Alex has one extra ticket to a ball game and two best friends. He took John last time so he decides to ask James. As he is asking James, John walks up.

CONFLICT

CONFLICT

Kim is talking to Alexis at lunch. All of a sudden, Sam comes up and asks Alexis to come talk with her. Alexis just walks away from Kim without saying goodbye.

CONFLICT

CONFLICT

Robert has been working hard on math all week. But when he gets his test back there is a D on it. While he is looking at the test, he hears other kids laughing.

CONFLICT

CONFLICT

Tish wants to go to the mall with her best friend. But her mom says she has to finish her homework first. Tish yells at her mom and is grounded for a week.

CONFLICT

Unit Summary for Group Leaders

In the introduction, we emphasized that this curriculum is designed to help children learn to stop and think before they act. The focus of unit 1 has been to enable children to stop and recognize their own feelings. The lessons teach children how to recognize, identify, and label up to eight common emotions. We emphasized that people feel (and show) emotions with words, with their faces, and with their bodies, and also that people often feel different degrees of emotions. The unit is designed to introduce several basic strategies that will help children stop during a social encounter and think actively about how they are feeling. These strategies—in particular, self talk—will prepare children to learn, practice, and apply the *Making Choices* skills that are introduced in future units.

In the next unit, we introduce the first step in solving social problems, encoding of cues. Many of the cues encountered in social situations will arise from the feelings and affect that are present in the situation. A good deal of the material we present in unit 2 therefore proceeds directly from concepts in unit 1.

UNIT 2: ENCODING: IDENTIFYING SOCIAL CLUES

Encoding is the first of six steps in the *Making Choices* problem-solving sequence. It refers to a child's ability to recognize and read the many social cues encountered in social situations, and, from the wide range of cues present, to select those cues that are relevant.

The goal of this unit is to increase the child's ability to recognize an array of social cues, ranging from subtle to overt, with an emphasis on the sequencing of cues in social situations.

Research has shown that children who use aggression are likely to miss many important social cues, skipping over subtle nuances and sequences of cues in favor of more memorable and exciting cues (Crick & Dodge, 1994; Dodge, Petitt, Bates, & Valente, 1995; Lochman & Dodge, 1994). One study found that, when compared to nonaggressive peers, boys identified as aggressive paid greater attention to social cues arising from aggressive interactions than to cues from benign or friendly interactions (Gouze, 1987). Another study revealed that boys diagnosed as both aggressive and hyperactive were able to recall significantly fewer social cues from hypothetical situations, when compared with boys in a normal control group, and, to a lesser extent, with boys who were hyperactive only or aggressive only (Milich & Dodge, 1984). In both of these studies, a boy's overall intelligence level was not found to influence attention to or recall of social cues. A third study found that aggressive and antisocial adolescents, when compared to nonaggressive adolescents, sought fewer additional facts about hypothetical situations (Slaby & Guerra, 1988).

Lesson 1: Situations and Cues

OBJECTIVE

Students will be able to provide developmentally appropriate definitions for *social cue* (K-6) and *social situation* (grades 4-6). Moreover, they will be able to give several simple examples of each.

REVIEW

Briefly summarize the material in the first unit, including the feelings you presented and discussed, how people might express them, and how feelings can vary in degree in different situations or social contexts. Remind students about the need to be able to figure out how they are feeling during a situation and how self-talk can help them stop, relax, and calm down so they can think.

ACTIVITIES

1. Remind students of the overall purpose of *Making Choices* (that is, to teach skills that will help them get along with peers and adults). Emphasize that they will now begin to learn about a series of skills they can use that will help them do this. (Make sure young children have some idea what a series, or sequence, is. One simple way to do this is to draw a poster of a set of stairs, with a child at the bottom and some prize or goal at the top. Each step of the staircase is one of the skills they will be learning in *Making Choices*.)

2. For older students, introduce the word *situation* and ask them for a definition. A dictionary definition would be *a combination of circumstances at a particular time and place.* The important idea is that a situation refers to the way things are (or what's going on) at a particular time and, usually, at a particular place. A *social situation* involves two or more people. For younger children, don't worry about providing a definition. Instead, tell the students they will be hearing some very short stories and seeing some pictures from magazines, and that you will be asking them to think about, for each, "What's going on here?"

3. Provide simple examples of different situations students might encounter during the day, such as:

- James walks into the classroom and

Materials

- List of simple social situations (see below)
- Poster showing the *Making Choices* problem-solving steps (see Figure 4, the staircase poster)

Group Process Tip: This lesson introduces a number of new concepts. Pay attention to how much content your group or class is able to understand. Keep relating content to group goals. Be careful not to overload children—it's OK to stretch this lesson over two sessions. Also, engage group members in taking leadership roles as much as possible. When you are describing common social situations, you might encourage students to generate examples themselves.

sees Louis playing with his favorite toy.

- Sadie looks up from her desk to find the teacher and all the other kids looking at her, waiting for her to say something, and she didn't even hear a question.
- Bob is walking down the hall after lunch and sees his best friend laughing with a kid who always tries to get other kids in trouble.
- Antonio is walking home from school and sees a group of boys wearing colors and walking toward him.

4. Describe to students how we come across many situations every day. Most situations are easy to figure out and we don't pay much attention to them. Sometimes, however, there's something about a situation that we don't understand or that we think needs to change. In these situations, it is a good idea to stop and think about what's going on.

5. Introduce the concept of a cue. You might describe the cues in a social situation as clues—like those in a mystery story or a puzzle—that give us more information about what is going on. A cue can be anything about the situation, such as the location or setting, who is present, what people are saying, how they are dressed, what their bodies are doing, and so on. Cues can come from other people or things, and they can also come from inside ourselves, such as a funny feeling in the stomach

that tells us we're upset or nervous. Ask students for the cues, or clues, that were present in one or two of the situations described earlier. For example, what were the cues that told Sadie that the teacher had probably just asked her a question?

6. Remind students of the feelings discussed in unit 1 and how they learned to identify their own feelings in a certain situation. Note that it can also be important to figure out how other people are feeling in the situation. For example:

Imagine that another student in your class walks up to you in the hall and bumps into you. This makes you a little bit mad. How is the other student feeling? Is she angry? Is she in a good mood and just playing around? Maybe she is sad about something and not paying attention.

7. Let students know that in the next lesson they will begin to look for the cues in a situation that can help them figure out how others are feeling. This can be very important information in trying to decide what's going on.

8. Introduce the idea that we also need to be aware of how our own feelings may be influencing what cues we notice and how much we pay attention to them. For example, ask students: "If you are very angry, do you think you would be more likely or less likely to notice how other people are feeling?"

SUMMARIZE THE MAIN IDEA

We can look for cues, or clues, in social situations, to answer the question: What's going on?

LESSON ENRICHMENT ACTIVITY

Have two students act out a role play (or puppet show) depicting a simple social situation. Ask the other students to name some of the cues present. After each situation, switch off so that everyone gets a turn acting and several turns watching for cues.

Lesson 2: Matching Feelings with Tone of Voice

OBJECTIVE

Children will improve their ability to identify feelings by listening to the tone of a person's voice.

Materials

- Plain paper plates (four for each child) and markers or crayons.

- Tape recorder and a tape with prerecorded words spoken in a way that suggests specific feelings such as happiness, sadness, anger, or fear (When recording, select common words that do not ordinarily imply specific feelings. For example, you might say "chair" with a "frightened" voice or "apple" with an "angry" voice. Pause for about ten seconds between each word when recording.)

REVIEW

Ask students to name the feelings discussed in unit 1. Spend several minutes making facial expressions, identifying body responses, and describing specific situations that correspond to the feelings while prompting students to match feelings. Examples: "How are people usually feeling when they cry?" "How are people feeling when they do this?" (the group leader smiles) and "When I don't get a turn on the trampoline I feel . . ."

ACTIVITIES

1. Ask students to draw one face on each paper plate, corresponding to the following feelings: happy, sad, angry, and frightened. Point out that today's lesson will focus on these four feelings only. For younger students you may wish to limit the discussion to two or three feelings.

2. Start the tape after explaining to students that they will need to listen carefully to each word. After each word is heard, turn off the recorder and ask students to hold up the face they think best represents the feeling being conveyed.

3. To modify this activity for older students, use regular paper instead of paper plates, and have them write out the feelings instead of drawing feeling faces. Instead of prerecording words, have the students pronounce them. Begin by preparing a collection of words beforehand, each written on a separate slip of paper, and place these in a container such as a basket or hat. Prepare another set of paper slips, each with the name of a particular feeling written on it, and place these in a separate container. Have students (perhaps beginning with one or two "leaders") take turns selecting a word out of one hat and a feeling out of the second hat. Ask the student to turn away from the group or to go behind a wall or bulletin board and pronounce the word several times, using a tone of voice that

Group Process Tip: The activity in this lesson is likely to produce giggles and silly comments. This is fine—remember, *Making Choices* is supposed to be fun—but make sure the fun is not interfering with learning. Remind members of the group the rules to which they have agreed. Also, have you checked in with the students' parents or teachers lately, to let them know what's going on in the group or to solicit their support? Doing so may increase the benefits for the students.

expresses the selected feeling. Ask the other students to hold up the paper with the feeling they think the student's tone of voice represented.

4. Have students check their responses with one another to see whether they agree about the emotion expressed. Ask students to discuss what they heard.

5. Remind students that their feelings in a situation might influence what they hear in the situation.

6. Listen to other words one at a time, pausing after each word, to allow for discussion. Encourage students to use self-talk to help them think about what the person's tone of voice is telling them.

SUMMARIZE THE MAIN IDEA

Many times we can tell how a person is feeling by listening to his or her tone of voice.

LESSON ENRICHMENT ACTIVITY

Have a student pick a piece of paper out of a hat. There should be a word on each paper, accompanied by either a happy, sad, frightened, or angry face. Instruct the student to decide which feeling the face is expressing, then have the student say the word in a way that expresses the feeling. The other children should try to guess the feeling. Be sure to discuss why students guessed as they did. Point out facial expressions, tone of voice, and body language.

Lesson 3: Noticing Multiple Cues

OBJECTIVE

Children will be able to notice and pay attention to a greater number and variety of cues when they encounter a social situation.

Materials

This lesson includes a menu of games that you might play with students. See the list of games at the end of the lesson for the materials that you will need.

REVIEW

Go around the circle and ask students to describe a simple situation that they encountered this week. Have the next person try to identify how the speaker might have felt and how others in the situation were feeling.

ACTIVITIES

1. Tell students that they are going to learn about other kinds of cues that may be present in a situation. The cues they have looked for so far have had to do with how others in the situation are feeling. Today students will be playing some games that involve paying attention and noticing, and they will also be learning about other kinds of cues that can tell them other things about the situation.

2. Play one of the games described below. Choose the game that seems most appropriate for the ages and interests of your group. Repeat the game or try different games.

3. To downplay competition, give students rewards both for winning and for active participation. In some way, recognize every student.

4. Between games, link the idea of being observant with self-talk. Ask students how they might use self-talk to notice more cues in a situation. Also, ask students to pretend they're frightened or sad during some of the games, and to tell the group how their feelings affected what they noticed and paid attention to.

5. Emphasize to students that often they can learn a great deal about a situation by taking a minute or two to look around and observe the cues or clues. For example, one important thing they can learn from noticing cues is whether a situation is safe or dangerous. Ask students to come up with some other important things they might learn by noticing cues.

6. Ask students to practice noticing, that is, observing situations actively, over the next week. For example, they might take five minutes after eating lunch to observe the cafeteria. Can they notice something they'd never noticed before (for example, an object, a way they do things, and so on)?

Group Process Tip: Encourage all members to participate in the games of this lesson. Try to draw out students who seem reluctant or shy. Help overly enthusiastic students learn to take turns. Make sure everyone is included and that everyone gets rewards for positive contributions.

SUMMARIZE THE MAIN IDEA

By being observant, we can notice more and different kinds of cues in situations. This helps us figure out what's going on.

GAMES

- "I Spy": Select one person to be "it." The student who is "it" chooses an object in the room that is in plain sight and informs the others of its color ("I spy something red"). The other students take turns guessing which object was chosen. Whoever guesses correctly chooses the next object. Group leaders can step in and appoint a new person "it" as needed, to make sure everyone gets a turn.
- Pick a common object from the room, such as a blackboard eraser or a small dictionary. Have one student leave the classroom. Select a second student to put the object somewhere in the room, in plain sight. Bring the first student back into the room, and have him or her search for the object. This student should describe the different objects he or she sees around the room in the search for the "hidden" object.
- Place an assortment of fairly small objects in a box. Include a mix of identical, similar, and unlike objects. For example, you might include a seashell, four playing cards, some blank three-by-five cards, some paper clips, a ball, a washcloth, two handkerchiefs, and so on. There

should be at least 20 objects in the box. Gently pour them out onto a table and let students examine them for a couple of minutes. Have one or two students leave the area, and remove four or five objects. Bring the student(s) back and ask them to identify which objects are missing. Repeat the process several times, allowing all students a chance to play. Discuss with students which objects were easier to identify as missing (for example, were unlike objects easier to spot as missing, relative to identical objects?) and why (for example, it was hard to remember whether there were three or four cards, but it was easy to spot that the ball was missing). Point out that different students are likely to notice different objects missing for different reasons.

- You can try a variation of the "I Spy" game with pictures cut out of magazines. Divide the students into two groups and provide each with an action picture from a magazine. Have them work together to write a list of all the cues or clues (objects, actions, people) they see in the picture. Each item on the list can be worth a certain number of points, which can be tied into the group's token system (ten points earn an extra token, for example).
- With very young children you might wish to use hidden object puzzles out of children's magazines. Another idea would be to watch a short video of children acting out common situations.

Lesson 4: Sequences of Cues

OBJECTIVE

Children will be able to notice, pay attention to, and describe the sequence of cues encountered in a social situation.

Materials

- Paper and pencils

Note: In this lesson, we present concepts and describe activities designed to increase students' awareness that cues occur sequentially in a social situation. Such awareness can help students understand where and how a particular cue fits in the context of the social situation. This realization may represent an initial formulation, by the child, of the meaning of the cue. Conceptually, this lesson could have been included in unit 3, because it highlights the link between the order of cues and their meaning. It appears in this unit instead because it also emphasizes two important skills that are presented and developed in other lessons in this unit: (1) noticing and (2) paying attention to the sequence of cues encountered in social situations. These skills are critical for successful cognitive problem solving at this step.

REVIEW

Go around the circle and ask each student to describe a setting they observed since the previous session. Did they notice new things about the setting? What were they? If a student does not complete this activity, ask that student to think of a setting with which he or she is familiar, such as the classroom or his or her room at home. Ask the student to think of and tell the group about the cues that are present in the setting. Prompt the student to generate multiple cues by asking open-ended (for example, "What else is there?") and direct questions ("Is there any more furniture? Describe it."). Remind students of the importance of taking time to notice multiple cues to obtain as much information as possible about a situation and what is going on.

ACTIVITIES

1. Introduce the concepts of *order* and *sequence* in developmentally appropriate language. For example, with young children, you might say something such as, "Usually, when things happen, they don't all happen at the same time. Instead, one thing happens first, then something else happens, then a third thing happens, and so on. When several things happen, one after the other, we call this a *sequence*."

2. Provide several simple examples, and then ask students to give examples. Examples might be:

Group Process Tip: Think about the group or class from a group development perspective. Do norms and roles seem to be emerging? Are members becoming engaged with each one another? Do you need to go over the goals of the group again or remind students of group rules? Soon some students should begin to use the system of rewards without prompts from you.

- First I woke up, then I got out of bed, then I walked to the kitchen, then I made breakfast.
- The first thing Louis did when he got to school was to say "hello" to his teacher. Then he hung up his jacket. Then he got out the Legos. Then he started to build a tower.
- Sadie did her math homework first thing. Then she had a snack, and then she went outside to play.

3. With older children you might point out that the alphabet and the numbers used for counting are sequences. With all students, discuss numerous examples and use plenty of phrases such as "first, then" or "before I did this, I had to do that" to highlight the concept of order.

4. Explain to students that a sequence might be made up of a series of actions, events, or cues (clues). Point out that most (perhaps all) actions, events, and cues are part of a sequence. For example, a single cue is usually preceded by some other cue, and will be followed by yet another cue. Very few cues (actions, events) occur in isolation.

5. Have students illustrate the idea of a sequence by drawing a series of simple pictures depicting the steps of a process (for example, getting ready for school, playing a game of baseball, or going to the store). Have students number each picture consecutively to emphasize which step happens first. You may need to provide an example, such as a

sequence of pictures showing
    1. someone asleep in bed
    2. an alarm clock going off
    3. the person getting dressed
    4. the person eating breakfast.

6. Remind students that problem solving involves a sequence and illustrate the idea with the staircase diagram.

7. Ask students to think about why it might be important to understand sequences. Focus the discussion on noticing cues in a social situation. Point out that the cues we notice are almost always part of a sequence of cues. Sometimes we have seen (heard, felt) what came before a particular cue, and other times we have not. Whenever we have not seen what came before a particular cue, it is important to stop and think and to ask ourselves, using self talk, "What might have happened before I came in?"

8. Give an example of why this question would be important to ask in a social situation. (As you introduce this idea, you are beginning to ask the question, "What does this mean?" which, as noted above, anticipates the next unit.) For example,

James walks into the classroom and sees Louis swinging a baseball bat. Suppose this is all James knows about the situation. What will he think is going on? Now suppose that when he sees Louis with the bat, James somehow finds out that, right before he came into the

room, the teacher asked Louis to show her his batting technique. What will James think is going on now?

9. Emphasize that finding out how and where a cue fits in a sequence can provide important information about a social situation. Students should practice thinking about cues by using self-talk to ask themselves questions such as "What happened before I came in? How can I find out?" Group leaders can also mention that this information will help them with the next step in cognitive problem solving, that is, thinking about what this means.

SUMMARIZE THE MAIN IDEA

The cues in a social situation usually occur in a sequence and not all alone. When we encounter a social cue, it is important to stop and think about what might have happened just before that cue. This can help us figure out how the cue fits in a sequence, which will help us understand what's going on and what it means.

LESSON ENRICHMENT ACTIVITY

Have the students play a game whereby they generate a story (a sequence of events). Ask one student to describe a character and an initial action. The next student in the circle describes the second action of the character, and so on around the circle of students. The actions of the character should fit together in some fashion, but need not be completely logical. The group leader may set up an initial scenario for the students, saying, for example, "Tell a story about a girl who has found a wallet with ten dollars,"or "Tell a story about a boy who wants to learn how to sail a boat."

Unit Summary for Group Leaders

In unit 2 we presented the idea that, in a social situation, children can observe cues that will help them figure out what is going on. Cues are like the clues in a puzzle or mystery. Many cues provide information about how the people in the situation are feeling. Children can learn how others are feeling by noticing cues such as tone of voice and body language, and by paying attention to what the people are doing. Children can learn other things from noticing cues, such as whether the situation is safe.

Cues may mean one thing in one social setting and quite another thing in a different setting. For example, encountering a group of boys with a baseball bat on the playground might be quite different from encountering a group of boys with bats on the street. Children should be encouraged to notice as many cues as possible. In general, it is a good idea to take the time to stop and actively observe the cues that are present in a social situation.

At this point, children have learned skills that will help them stop and think about how they are feeling. They have also learned to observe and pay attention to a variety of cues that are present in a social situation. In the next unit, they will use cues to draw inferences about the intent of others and learn skills designed to help them interpret the cues in a situation. *Interpretation of cues*, the second step in the *Making Choices* program, is an important part of thinking about what is going on before acting.

UNIT 3: INTERPRETATION: MAKING SENSE OF SOCIAL CLUES

The second step in the *Making Choices* program is *interpretation*. Interpretation refers to the processes by which children assign meaning to social cues. These processes include (a) using schemas and heuristics, (b) making inferences about causality, (c) attributing intent to others, and (d) assessing the effectiveness of one's own previous efforts to problem solve in the current situation. Interpretation involves assessing cues from a current social situation on the basis of previous experiences (including earlier social interactions, past relationships, prior exposure to similar situations, and so on). It can also involve recognizing novel cues and creating new meanings for them (for example, different categories or subcategories, gradations of existing categories, integration of multiple concepts) (Crick & Dodge,

The goal of this unit is to increase each child's ability to identify social cues and to label them accurately, as either friendly or hostile, intentional or unintentional.

1994). Accurate assessment of social cues is essential for creating and implementing an effective strategy for social interaction and for productive problem solving.

Many research studies have shown that children who are impulsive, oppositional, or who use aggression have difficulty interpreting cues accurately, and they are likely to perceive benign (and, at times, friendly) situations as threatening or hostile. Consequently, they are more likely to respond aggressively. Their failure to interpret social cues accurately is thought to be one reason for their hostile style of interaction (see, for example, Dodge, Price, Bachorowski, & Newman, 1990; Lochman & Dodge, 1994; Milich & Dodge, 1984; Quiggle et al., 1992; Slaby & Guerra, 1988).

Lesson 1: Recognizing Others' Intentions

OBJECTIVE

Children will learn to identify and distinguish friendly and hostile (or mean) intentions in others. For older students you might also present and discuss ambivalent ("can't tell") intentions.

Materials

- Activity sheet 11 and scissors
- Two puppets (K-3)
- Situation scenarios (examples are provided, although group leaders may need to modify or construct additional scenarios that are appropriate for your group)
- Cartoon situations (provided below)

REVIEW

Ask students to recall the different ways we can tell what a person is feeling (facial expressions, body language, tone of voice). Encourage them to give examples. Review the idea of cues (or clues), talking about detectives, what they do, and how they look for clues to help them solve mysteries or puzzles. Remind students that facial expression, body language, and tone of voice are all clues that help us figure out how a person is feeling. Feelings can also affect the cues we notice and pay attention to. Also caution students to remember that they may have missed some important cues in a situation, and if so it's important to find out what happened.

ACTIVITIES

1. Pass out scissors and activity sheet 11 to each student. Have students cut out the faces on the worksheet. (Each face represents one intention.) Ask students to describe how the faces might be feeling. Encourage them to identify the clues that led to their answers. For older students, you may just want to show a copy of the sheet to students to serve as a guide to intentions.

2. Introduce younger students to the two puppets and explain that these puppets are going to help them practice reading clues. Have older children act out the scenes in role plays. Tell the students to watch each scene carefully, and instruct them to hold up the face that best describes the intentions of the puppets (actors) at the end of each scene. (*Note: Group leaders should create scenes commonly encountered in school, at home, and in the neighborhood. Situations should be simple, involving only one interaction.*)

Group Process Tip: Remember to help students "step out of their roles," especially difficult emotional or interpersonal ones, in any role plays you use in this lesson. Remind students that the situations they acted out were made up to help them learn about deciding what's going on in a situation.

3. Group leaders should have puppets or students act out each scene twice, demonstrating the intentions *friendly* and *hostile* (add *ambivalent*, or "can't tell," for older students). As appropriate, have the puppets (or encourage the actors to) engage in self-talk. After each scene, ask students to

indicate which intention was depicted in the scene. Ask them to describe the clues that helped them arrive at their decision. Compare and contrast scenes using specific examples that help children see the differences between intentions more clearly.

4. During one set of scenes, have one puppet (or actor) pretend he or she is very happy about getting a new toy earlier in the day or getting tickets to a big concert. Does this change how the puppet or actor interprets the actions of the other character in the scene?

5. An alternative activity, especially for older students, uses the set of cartoons found at the end of this lesson. Show students the first cartoon, or pass a copy around the group. Ask students to identify whether the cues in the cartoon (for example, the actions, words, or expressions) indicate hostile, friendly, or ambivalent intentions. Have students describe how they chose an intention and which cues helped them figure out what was going on. Be sure that they attend to cues that are individual (tone of voice, for example) and contextual (for example, whether adult supervision is present). Repeat this exercise for each cartoon. After presenting the last cartoon, summarize (or have students summarize) how students decided on the intentions of the cartoon characters. Point out that several cartoons could be hostile or friendly, depending on the caption. For

most of the cartoons, it would have been difficult to interpret the intention had there not been a caption.

SUMMARIZE THE MAIN IDEA

People's intentions can be either friendly or hostile. We can often tell people's intention by their words, their tone of voice, their actions, and what is going on around them.

LESSON ENRICHMENT ACTIVITY

Using magazines and newspapers, cut out pictures of people with friendly or hostile expressions engaged in social situations. Divide the class into small groups of two or three and pass out several pictures to each group. Instruct students to separate the friendly pictures from the hostile ones. (Students can create a collage with the separate groups of pictures.) Ask students to identify the clues that helped them decide which pictures were positive and which were negative. List the clues on a board and review the differences between friendly and hostile interactions.

SCENES

Presented on the next page are sample scenes or scenarios. These can be modified to fit the developmental level of your group, or you can create new scenes appropriate for your group. You can also use situations that students have generated in earlier lessons to develop other scenes. Be sure to alter the setting—home, school, and neighborhood—so students can learn to assess the context of cues in making interpretations.

- Puppet (Actor) #1 is watching TV at home.
  Hostile: Puppet #2 comes in, pushes past him, and changes the channel.
  Friendly: Puppet #2 comes in and asks if he can watch TV too. Puppet #1 agrees. Puppet #2 asks if he can pick the next program when this show is over. Puppet #1 says, "Sure!"
  Can't Tell: Puppet #1 is watching TV. Puppet #2 comes in, walks around the room a few times, says nothing, finally stops, and stares at the TV while blocking the view of Puppet #1.

- You are skateboarding down a hill. As you get to the bottom, a boy from your class rides his bike right in front of you, causing you to fall onto the hard pavement. You lie on the street in great pain.
  Hostile: The boy looks at you and laughs and then keeps on riding down the street.
  Friendly: The boy gets off his bike, runs over to you, and asks if you're okay.
  Can't Tell: The boy rides off without looking at you (did he even see you?).

- You are in the bathroom at school combing your hair in front of the mirror. There are several other people in the bathroom. A person walks out of the stall, looks at you and comments,
  Hostile: "Your new haircut looks horrible on you!"
  Friendly: "I like your hair."
  Can't Tell: "Oh, I see you got a haircut."

- You get on the school bus at the end of the day. The bus is very crowded.
  Friendly: As you walk down the aisle looking for a seat, you see a boy move over in his seat, leaving room on his seat near the aisle.
  Hostile: You see an empty seat but the kid behind you pushes you out of the way and grabs the seat. He looks up at you and says, "Tough luck, zit-face."
  Can't Tell: You see an empty seat but just as you're heading for it a kid who was standing at the back of the bus walks forward and takes the seat.

- You are in the movie theater waiting in line to buy popcorn and a soda. As you wait, you look around and see that the new boy from your class is also at the theater. He looks up and sees you.
  Friendly: He smiles and waves to you.
  Hostile: The boy shoots his middle finger at you.
  Can't Tell: The boy turns and walks in the other direction.

- You are walking down the hallway at school and you see a friend of yours walking toward you. You wave and call out her name.

  Can't Tell: She continues walking without responding to you.

  Friendly: Your friend runs over and asks you if you've seen Leo's new movie.

  Hostile: She tells you that she's been invited to a big party, and then laughs and tells you that you weren't invited.

- Your friend gets a new video game for his birthday. He asks another boy to come over after school and play a game with him.

  Can't Tell: He does not ask you to come over to his house to play.

  Hostile: He tells you that you're the last person he'd want to play with the video game because you're too dumb to figure out electronic games.

  Friendly: Your friend tells you that he can only have one person over at a time, and he would like you to come try out the video game next week.

CARTOON 1

"So, after we write the fake love letter and put it on Ms. Smith's desk, then we'll tell everyone that Jack is in love with her. He'll be so embarrassed."

CARTOON 2

"You guys are the best friends I've ever had!"

CARTOON 3

"I like to mow Grandma's lawn for her. She is always so pleased when I help her out."

CARTOON 4

"I'm going to mow down all of Mom's flowers because she won't let me go to Fred's house tonight."

CARTOON 5

"Shhhh! Be very quiet!"

CARTOON 6

The audience calls out, "Bravo! You did a wonderful job!"

CARTOON 7

The audience calls out, "Boo! Sit down! You stink!"

CARTOON 8

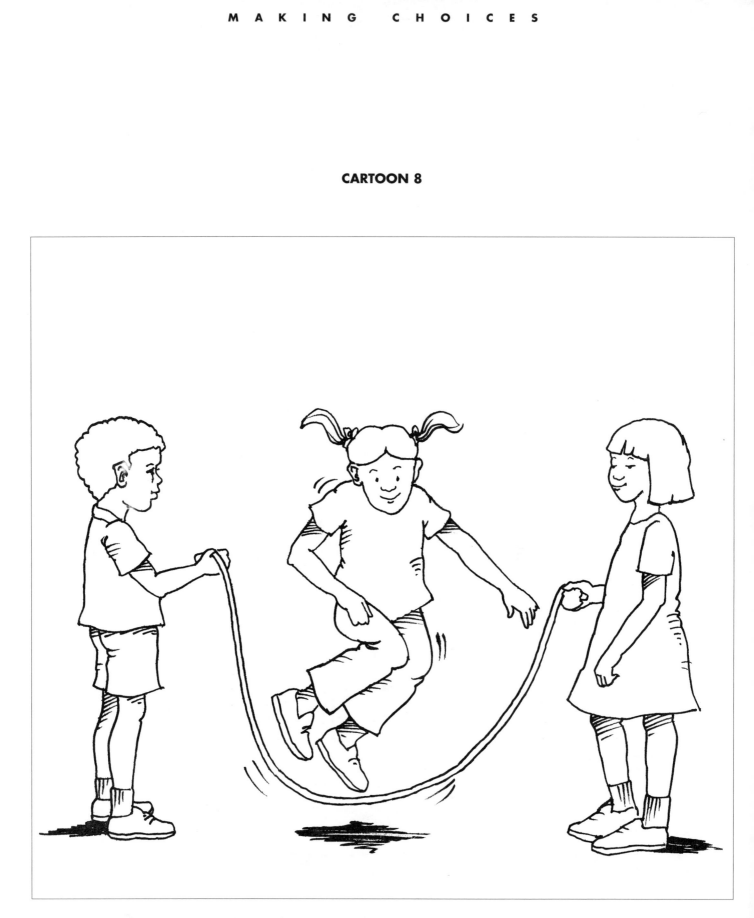

The girl on the right says to the boy, "You can go next. I'll wait.
I don't mind turning the rope for a while."

CARTOON 9

"Ha, ha, you guys fell in the mud. Everybody's gonna make fun of you."

85

ACTIVITY SHEET 11

**On Purpose
to be Friendly**

**On Purpose
to be Mean**

**Can't Tell
??????**

Lesson 2: Distinguishing Intentions

OBJECTIVE

Children will improve their ability to recognize and talk about the difference between friendly and hostile intentions. They will also be able to distinguish when an action is *intentional* (on purpose) or *unintentional* (accidental).

Materials

- Friendly, accidental, and hostile tic-tac-toe game sheets and game tokens (activity sheet 12) (Several sample game sheets are provided, and you can make up additional ones as needed. Make enough copies of the token sheets and cut out enough single tokens so that each student has an adequate amount.)

REVIEW

Review the previous lesson, asking students to recall the friendly and hostile ways in which the puppets interacted. Ask students to identify the clues that helped them see differences in how the puppets acted. Review ambivalent (can't tell) intentions, if you covered them.

ACTIVITIES

1. Introduce the idea of *intentional* versus *unintentional* behavior. Point out that this is another way to think about the reasons for someone's behavior. Discuss with students that a single action could be the result of very different intentions. Provide a simple example, such as:

"A boy bumps into you on the playground." His intentions might have been either of the following:

- Unintentional: He bumped you because he was trying to catch a ball and didn't see you.
- Intentional: He bumped you because he was mad at you.

2. You can use words like *on purpose* and *by accident* (or *mistake*) with younger children. Ask students to give examples of things they have done unintentionally. Remember to mention how someone's feelings might influence how they understand someone's intent (for example, "If I'm already angry, will I decide he bumped me by accident or on purpose?").

3. Hand out the tic-tac-toe sheets and tokens. Explain that you will be calling out behaviors that are written on the sheets you gave them (read off the sheets or create a separate list for yourself). Children who have a behavior listed on their boards should mark over the behavior with a smile face, a mad face, or an "uh-oh" face. Draw examples on the board and explain that the three faces correspond to friendly, hostile, and accidental interactions. When children get three of the same faces in a row, they should raise their hands and call off their lists.

Group Process Tip: Keep examining where the group is in terms of its development. Do what you can to help members build the group's sense of community and purpose (and to have members use group rules).

4. Repeat the game several times, using new game boards. You can make different bingo cards covering a wide variety of situations. Be sure that every board has at least one "winning sequence," that is, three behaviors with the same intention shown in a row, column, or diagonally. Modify as needed for older students by including "can't tell" behaviors (note that some of the behaviors in the examples provided could be of this type).

LESSON ENRICHMENT ACTIVITY

Read the story *Foolish Rabbit's Big Mistake*, by Rafe Martin and Ed Young. This is a story about a rabbit who misreads cues and begins to believe the world is ending.

ACTIVITY SHEET 12

LAUGHS WITH YOU	HITS YOU	SHARES WITH YOU
MAKES A FACE AT YOU	HUGS YOU	IGNORES YOU
TALKS ABOUT YOU	BITES YOU	HELPS YOU

ACTIVITY SHEET 12

CALLS YOU A NAME	LIES TO YOU	MAKES YOU FALL
TELLS ON YOU	SMILES AT YOU	BLAMES YOU
PLAYS WITH YOU	TELLS YOU TO BE QUIET	SMILES AT YOU

ACTIVITY SHEET 12

PUSHES YOU	MAKES YOU CRY	CALLS YOU NAMES
HURTS YOU	MAKES YOU FALL	RUNS INTO YOU
SHARES WITH YOU	SMILES AT YOU	TELLS YOU A SECRET

ACTIVITY SHEET 12

MAKES A FACE AT YOU	BITES YOU	IGNORES YOU
TELLS YOU A JOKE	TEASES YOU	PLAYS WITH YOU
TELLS YOU TO BE QUIET	ASKS YOU FOR HELP	STARES AT YOU

ACTIVITY SHEET 12—GAME TOKENS

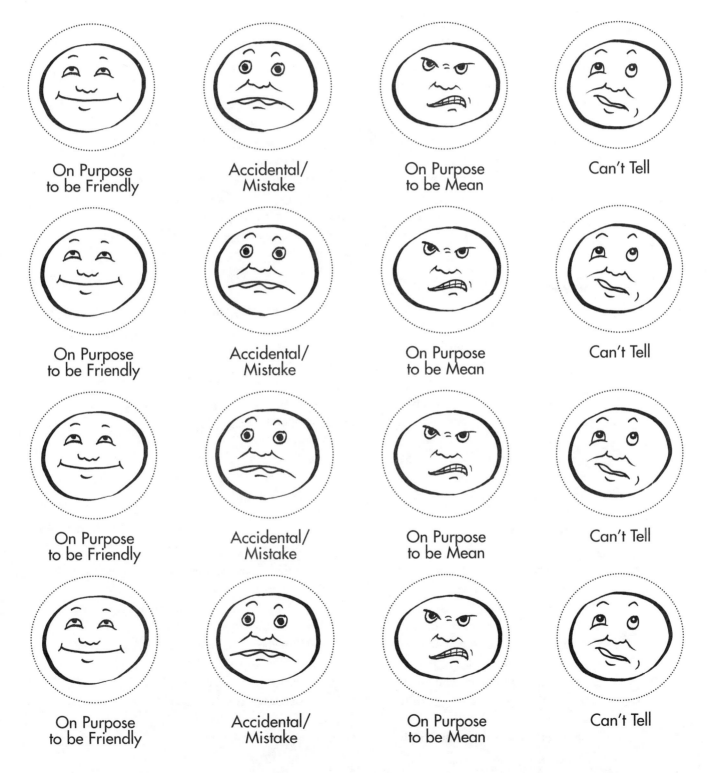

On Purpose to be Friendly

Accidental/ Mistake

On Purpose to be Mean

Can't Tell

On Purpose to be Friendly

Accidental/ Mistake

On Purpose to be Mean

Can't Tell

On Purpose to be Friendly

Accidental/ Mistake

On Purpose to be Mean

Can't Tell

On Purpose to be Friendly

Accidental/ Mistake

On Purpose to be Mean

Can't Tell

Lesson 3: Distinguishing Intentional and Unintentional Behavior

OBJECTIVE

Children will improve their ability to use clues from a situation to identify correctly whether the behavior of others is *intentional* or *unintentional* and whether an intention is *hostile* or *friendly*. Children will also improve their ability to encode a greater number of cues from a social situation.

Materials

- Activity sheet 13: Stories for the detective game or the jury game (two samples are provided)

REVIEW

Review previous lessons, emphasizing the ways in which we distinguish a friendly situation from a hostile one. Describe clues, including facial expressions, body language, and tone of voice. Have students describe the ways in which the puppets or actors expressed their intentions. Remind students about how they can use self-talk when they are trying to interpret what cues mean.

ACTIVITIES

1. Ask students to think about why it is important to be able to identify whether a behavior is intentional or not. If students do not mention it, point out that knowing another person's intention helps us understand a social situation better and helps us decide what we should do next. Ask students whether they think an unintentional act is usually hostile, friendly, or neutral. Emphasize that, usually, unintentional acts are not hostile.

2. Select either the detective or jury game to play with students. The games are similar, but you play the detective game with the group as a whole, and you assign students to small groups to play the jury game. The detective game is probably more suitable for younger students and the jury game for older students. Each game uses the same stories and sets of clues.

3. After a couple of games, lead a general discussion with students. Points to emphasize include:

- It is important to pay attention to multiple cues, and, when possible, to all the cues in a situation. Doing so can help us figure out the intention of another person.
- Some clues are more important than others. That is, some clues tell us a great deal about a situation, and others tell us very little.
- In most situations, there are different kinds of cues or clues available (for example, in the second story on activity sheet 13, consider the actions

Group Process Tip: The games in this lesson provide an opportunity for students to model an important skill, i.e., waiting to find out all the facts before making an interpretation. Be sure to point out when students do this, and provide lots of positive feedback to them for doing so. Have them provide positive feedback to each other. Point out—and encourage students to point out—the benefits of finding out all the facts.

of Bob versus the "physical evidence").

- Making a decision too quickly about the intention of another can lead to an incorrect interpretation.
- Figuring out the intention of others helps us decide what we should do next.

Note: These games can improve children's interpretation and encoding skills. They encourage children to gather more information (encoding) before deciding what any one cue means (interpreting). In discussions, group leaders should try to elicit this point from students. The games also make clear a concept from social-cognition theory that was introduced at the beginning of this unit: Children's interpretation of cues is influenced by how their experience is represented in memory. To appreciate this point, look at the list of clues provided in the first story in activity sheet 13. They concern not only cues that are present in the immediate situation (for example, James is rubbing his elbow, which has a big bruise on it) but also a general opinion of James, based on experience over time (for example, James throws things when he gets angry).

SUMMARIZE THE MAIN IDEA

Sometimes people do things on purpose, and other times they might do the same thing by accident. We can often tell whether an act was intentional by looking for clues before we decide. Unintentional acts are usually not hostile.

LESSON ENRICHMENT ACTIVITIES

Select an excerpt from a video that depicts a social interaction between children of similar age and background as the group members. View the excerpt and lead a discussion about the intentions of the actors and clues that you might use to decide about intentions.

If you have a fairly large group of older students, divide them into two groups; have each group write a story and create a list of clues for a new round of the jury game. Then have each group play a round of the game with the story and clues of the other group.

ACTIVITY SHEET 13: GAMES

THE DETECTIVE GAME

This game is designed to help children learn to pay attention to all of the clues in a situation and to consider these clues before making an interpretation. In the game children get to be detectives who are looking for the clues about why a person has done something. You begin by telling students that they are going to be detectives, and they have to decide whether a person acted on purpose or unintentionally (by accident). Tell students that you will read them a short story. Then you will read a list of cues, or clues, that should help them figure out what is going on in the situation. They should listen to the clues and decide whether the person in the story acted on purpose—either to be mean or to be friendly—by accident or whether it's impossible to tell. Give each student a set of cards (provided). Tell students that they can make their decision at any time while you are reading the list of clues; they can listen to as few or as many clues as they like. When they have made a decision, they should place the card that reflects their decision on their desk or on the floor in front of them. Once they have made a decision, they must stick to it, even if they change their mind after hearing additional clues. You can simplify the game by having students decide between two cards, "On Purpose to be Mean" or "Accidental/Mistake."

Ask students whether they have any questions, then read the first story. Slowly read the clues, pausing for a moment between each. Note when each student makes his or her decision about the intention of the person in the story, and make sure no one tries to take back the card once he or she has reached a decision. When you have finished the list of clues, make sure all students have placed one of the cards in front of them. If some students have not done so, ask them to make up their mind now.

Lead a discussion with students about how and when they made their decision. Ask students who chose "On purpose" if they still believe the action was intentional, based on all the evidence. Point out that paying attention to all the available cues can help us make better decisions.

ACTIVITY SHEET 13: DETECTIVE GAME ANSWER CARDS

On Purpose to be Mean

On Purpose to be Friendly

By Accident or by Mistake

Can't Tell

ACTIVITY SHEET 13: GAMES

THE JURY GAME

The jury game is another activity designed to help children pay attention to all the cues in a situation before deciding whether someone's actions were intentional and hostile. In this game, children are the jury and decide whether the person in the story acted intentionally or by accident. Create several stories (two examples are provided), and a set of clues for each, with each clue written on a separate slip of paper. Before you read a story, place its set of clues in a box or hat so that students will be able to select four at random. Assign students to small groups and read the following instructions:

You are on a jury, and your assignment is to decide whether a person's behavior was intentional or unintentional. You will pick four clues, discuss the clues with your group, and come up with a verdict based on the clues you have. You will present your findings to the class, as well as the reasons for your decision.

Read the first story. Have the first group of students pick four clues, write them down without sharing them with the larger group, and place them back in the hat. Repeat so that each group has (potentially) a different set of clues—some groups will probably share one or two clues. Ask students to discuss the story and their set of clues as a group for about five minutes, and then to reach a verdict about whether the person acted on purpose or not. After groups have reached a verdict, ask students in each group to identify the clues they received, to report their verdict, and to explain why they reached their verdict. After all groups have presented their verdicts, review the entire list of clues with the larger group. Using all the clues, have the group try to agree on a final verdict. Ask students to identify the clues they think are most important and why. Point out that having the entire set of clues ("all the information") probably made it easier to reach a good decision about the intention of the person in the story.

ACTIVITY SHEET 13: GAMES

STORY 1

In art class, Phil made a clay sculpture that he really liked. After carefully placing the sculpture on the art table by the window, he left it to dry in the classroom. After lunch, Phil came back to class and discovered that his sculpture was broken to bits. James walked into class, looked at Phil, looked at the sculpture, and said, "I broke your artwork."

Based on your four clues, what's your verdict? Did James break the sculpture on purpose, or was it an accident?

(Cut out the clues for the jury game. Read them in order for the detective game.)

Phil and James got into an argument yesterday over kickball.	When Phil goes to tell the teacher, James asks to go to the bathroom.	James has paint on his shirt and face.	James throws things when he gets angry.
A couple of paintings on the art table are messed up.	James is really clumsy and bangs into things often.	There is a puddle of water on the floor beside the art table.	James is rubbing his elbow, which has a big bruise on it.
James says to Phil, "I'm really sorry. I didn't mean to break it."	James invited Phil to his birthday party earlier this morning.	James and Phil have been best friends since they were 5 years old.	Another kid comes in and says, "James, I'm sorry I bumped into you. Are you okay?"

ACTIVITY SHEET 13: GAMES

STORY 2

You worked really hard on your math homework. When you get to school, you carefully put your homework in your math book and leave the book on your desk before going over to the gym. When you get back from the gym, Bob is pulling your math book and homework out of a bucket full of soapy water. Bob looks at you and says, "Gee, it looks like I ruined your homework and your book."

(Cut out the clues for the jury game. Read them in order for the detective game.)

Bob sometimes does mean things so that other kids will think he's cool.	You and Bob got into an argument this morning over who could use the computer first.	Bob, another kid, and the teacher are the only other people in the room.	There are several jars of paint on the counter by your desk, right next to the window.
Yesterday Bob offered to help you with some math problems that were really hard.	When Bob saw your book and homework were ruined, he said, "Gee, that's too bad. I'm sorry."	There's a strong wind blowing in one of the windows beside your desk.	There is a bunch of paint spilled on the floor beside your desk.
There is a mop sitting on the floor beside Bob.	Bob has soap and water all over his shirt and pants.	The teacher tells you she asked Bob to mop beside your desk because some paint spilled.	Another kid tells you he bumped into Bob while Bob was mopping.

Lesson 4: Situations, Meanings, and Problems

OBJECTIVE

Children will be able to look at a situation, its cues and their meaning, and decide whether there is a problem.

Materials

- Flip chart and markers
- Activity sheet 14 and pencils

REVIEW

Ask students to explain how they might distinguish friendly from hostile situations and how they might recognize someone's intentions. Ask about all the cues they might look for, and what they mean. Encourage the use of self-talk.

ACTIVITIES

1. Introduce the word *problem*. Ask for definitions. This is one word with which most children will be familiar. Emphasize that there can be many different kinds of problems and many definitions of the word. Explain that, for the purpose of this group, there will be a special definition of the word.

2. Write the following definition on the flip chart: A problem is a situation where somebody thinks something needs to change.

3. If necessary, review the definition of situation in age-appropriate language. Encourage students to think about a situation they have discussed in earlier lessons. Was there something that needed to change? It could be a person (for example, his or her actions or words), a thing (for example, too much noise, not enough food), or a feeling (for example, being scared, being angry). What exactly needed to change? Encourage students to be specific.

4. Explain that if everything in a situation is okay and nothing needs to change, then there is no problem. When something does need to change, then it is important to stop and think about what exactly we think needs to change and why. Point out that not all the people in the situation might agree that something needs to change or on what needs to change. If there is disagreement, then there is a problem.

5. Point out to students that in some situations they might think that everything is okay, that nothing needs to change. But another person in the situation might think that they need to change.

Group Process Tip: Remember to take stock of your group on a regular basis—what roles are different members taking on and do these help or hinder task accomplishment? Is there a student who models proactive behavior and interaction? Does a particular student tend to get others "off track"? Use this information in planning activities and sub-groupings.

6. Have students fill out activity sheet 14 with respect to several simple situations. Two examples are provided, and you can use examples from previous lessons (for example, lesson 1 in unit 3). You can also create new situations or have students do so. You may wish to have older students break down into small groups

to fill out the activity sheet. Encourage students to think of a problem simply in terms of what needs to change.

SUMMARIZE THE MAIN IDEA

In a social situation, there is a problem if something needs to change.

SITUATIONS
(USE WITH ACTIVITY SHEET 14)

Martin hears Phil tell some other students that he is having a party next weekend. However, when Martin talks to Phil by himself, Phil mentions nothing about the party. Martin really wants to go the party and feels hurt that Phil did not say anything. Now Martin and Phil are waiting for the school bus on the playground after school.

When Jasmine is in a good mood she is able to do all of her chores on time and neatly. When she is in a bad mood, she hates doing her chores and often refuses to do them. Today she is in a bad mood and hasn't done one chore and her mother is coming through the front door.

ACTIVITY SHEET 14: PROBLEM CHECKLIST

THE PROBLEM: *WHAT* NEEDS TO CHANGE?	Who/What EXACTLY?	Why?	Who thinks so? Who doesn't?	Are there more clues or cues?
What somebody is *saying?*				
What somebody is *doing?*				
An object, such as the TV or the radio?				
The place? Is it safe? Is it ____?				
Something else?				

Unit Summary for Group Leaders

In this unit we have emphasized that children can interpret a social situation by determining whether others' behaviors are intentional or not and whether their intentions are hostile or friendly. There are certainly other ways in which people assign meaning to cues in social situations, but it is important that children be able to interpret these basic conditions. This helps them avoid potentially risky situations, and it also prevents them from seeing hostility where it does not exist. As we mentioned earlier, children who are aggressive are more likely to interpret ambiguous or friendly cues as hostile and to respond in kind. Using self-talk may be especially helpful for accurately interpreting others' intentions.

In part, accurate interpretation involves understanding cues in the context of the social and physical environment. Interpreting a look or a walk as hostile on the street may be appropriate (and may provide a margin of safety); however, in the school setting the same cue might call for a different interpretation. Children should develop skills in noticing cues and interpreting them in the context of the social situation.

Upon completion of unit 3, children have learned about feelings and practiced how to recognize feelings in themselves and others. They have learned to stop and think about what is going on in a social situation—that is,

what others are doing and what their actions, words, and other cues mean. The next step in the *Making Choices* program is for children to think about what they want to happen in the situation. That is, they need to formulate a goal.

UNIT 4: GOAL FORMULATION AND REFINEMENT: SETTING SOCIAL GOALS

Goal formulation is the third step in *Making Choices*. Once children have encoded and interpreted relevant cues in a social situation, they begin to formulate potential goals they wish to accomplish in the situation. The cognitive process of goal formulation is shaped by factors including socialization or modeling, cultural norms, past experiences, and emotional stability.

Research results suggest that children who have a strong sense of self-efficacy—of being effective in social situations—are more likely to formulate prosocial goals with positive long-term consequences, such as being better liked by peers (Rabiner & Coie, 1989; Slaby & Guerra, 1988). The ability to formulate and manage simultaneously multiple prosocial goals (for example, to become friends with a new student and remain friends with your best buddy) may be an especially important skill for social competence. Aggressive children, on the other hand, may be less able to formulate multiple goals, and more likely to think of goals that concern establishing and maintaining immediate feelings of control and dominance (Slaby & Guerra, 1988). They are likely to ignore long-term consequences in favor of instant gratification.

The goal of this unit is to enable children to formulate a greater number and variety of socially responsive prosocial goals when encountering social situations.

Lesson 1: What Is a Goal?

OBJECTIVE

Children will be able to distinguish a *goal* from an *action* used to obtain a goal. They will also be able to name three goals when presented with a description of a simple social situation.

Materials

- Activity sheet 15, flip chart, and marker
- Situation cards (described below)
- Pencils or markers and notebook paper
- Dictionary

REVIEW

Review units 1, 2, and 3 with students, emphasizing main points such as visual and verbal clues and the difference between friendly, neutral, and hostile intentions. One way to begin the review is to go around the group asking each student to think of one of the basic feelings. Each student should then demonstrate the feeling with his or her face and body. Have the others guess which feeling the student is demonstrating and talk about the clues they used to make their guess. Students can also act out a feeling in pairs. During the discussion, help students identify friendly, hostile, and ambiguous cues.

ACTIVITIES

1. Explain that the next step in problem solving involves thinking about and setting goals. Ask students if they know what a goal is. Read (or have a volunteer read) a dictionary definition.

2. Come up with a simple definition that everyone understands and write it on the flip chart. Ask for examples and write these down too. For example:

> *A goal is something a person wants to do or something a person would like to have. "Annie wants a new soccer ball," "Louis wants to buy a new basketball goal," "Sadie wants to have fun at a party," and "James wants to get an A on the test" are all goals.*

Point out that we set goals all the time by deciding what we want to accomplish. Often a goal involves getting something we don't have, but some goals involve wanting to keep something that we already have.

3. Group leaders can also talk about how a person can have more than one goal at a time, and that often we have to choose between goals. Sometimes we may believe we can have more than one goal, and if so we have to figure out a way to reach all of them.

4. Finally, emphasize that choosing a goal (wanting or needing something that

Group Process Tip: Be sure to monitor how well students understand the key ideas presented in this lesson. These ideas are central to much that comes later in the curriculum, and they relate directly to the group goals. Repeat the main ideas often, and check with students to find out whether they can state the ideas in their own words. Encourage students to take on task leadership roles if they can. Give lots of encouragement for incremental success and ask students to support and praise each other. You may need to spread this content over two sessions.

we don't have, or wanting to keep something that we do have) is separate from thinking about what we have to do to reach the goal, although we can think about both at the same time. During this discussion, you should keep in mind that it is often difficult to separate, in one's mind, a goal from the actions required to accomplish it. You will probably encounter this conceptual problem in planning and running this session, and it may even be apparent in some of the examples provided. Often there is a fine line between a goal and an action, and it may be impossible to determine with certainty where one stops and the other begins. Don't be too concerned if some of your goals sound a bit like focused actions, but avoid expressing goals strictly in terms of actions. The important point is for students to begin thinking about the distinction between what they want to accomplish and what they do to accomplish it and to realize that they are capable of coming up with more than one goal in problematic situations.

5. Read aloud one of the situation cards (see the examples on pages 109 and 110). Ask students to think about specific goals they might have in this situation. Provide an example or two if necessary, and then have the group generate a list of four or five possible goals for the situation.

6. Divide the group into smaller groups of two or three students each to repeat the situation card exercise. Give each group a different situation card, some notebook paper, and a pencil or marker. With older children, ask for a volunteer (or designate one student) in each small group to write down the group's responses. Instruct each small group to come up with three different goals they might have in their situation. Group leaders should rotate among the groups to monitor progress and help out if needed. Don't automatically facilitate for a group unless the students clearly need help. Make sure the designated student writes down the group's three goals (or do this yourself for younger students). Allow about five to 10 minutes for this exercise, and give the students a "two-minute warning" before calling time.

7. When all groups have three goals, the group leader should call on one student from each to read the situation card and goals. As each group makes its report, lead a discussion with the entire group about the goals that were formulated. Can students come up with additional goals? Ask students whether they have ever been in a similar situation, and, if so, what goal or goals did they generate? During this discussion, do not allow students to judge (criticize or praise) goals. Instead, focus on generating multiple goals.

8. Collect the situation card and goals from each group after they have been read aloud. Mention to the students that you will be asking them to read these again during the next session while you

tape them on a cassette recorder. (Be sure to keep each group's card and goal sheet together and to write on the sheets the names of the students who were in the group).

Example of goals (from the situation between Tom and John described in the cards)

- John wants to be friends with Tom.
- John would like to get back at Tom.
- John wants Tom to apologize.
- John hopes to be able to stay at Tom's home on Friday night.

  Note: Be sure to mention how emotions might influence goal formulation. We do not give specific examples in this unit, as we have done before, but rather encourage group leaders to discuss the role of emotions at appropriate times.

SUMMARIZE THE MAIN IDEA

A goal is something we want or need that we don't have now or something we want to keep. We set big and small goals all the time.

LESSON ENRICHMENT ACTIVITIES

1. Provide each student with drawing paper and crayons or markers. Describe a common classroom situation, and ask students to think of and write down two goals they might have in the situation. Have the students fold their paper in half and illustrate their choices.

2. Have students complete activity sheet 15. This sheet is appropriate for students age 10 years and over. (Correct answers: 1, 3, 4, 6, 7, and 9 are goals.

SITUATION CARDS

The student next to you copies off your paper.	You hear Annie telling another girl that she's not going to invite you to her birthday party.	Your best friend tells you she cheated on the social studies test yesterday.
You accidentally hit the meanest kid in class in the nose during a soccer or basketball game in gym class.	Jamie goes into your desk and takes your favorite pencil, without asking.	Tom tells everyone at school he heard John's parents fighting when he visited John's house yesterday.
You see Jennifer handing out invitations to her birthday party and you do not receive one.	You have tickets to see a great concert, but you don't know which of your two best friends to ask to come along.	You want to go hang out with your friend, but you just had an argument with your father and you need his permission to go.

SITUATION CARDS

Your buddy has to go home early, but you see a bunch of kids you don't know playing ball.	A new kid at school reaches for the last piece of cake in the cafeteria just as you were reaching for it.	Two friends you haven't seen in a while ask you if you want to check out the CDs they just swiped.
You are playing ball in the gym when an older kid tells you your haircut looks like dog fur.	Two guys you don't know seem to be following you home.	A guy you can't stand comes to school and tells everybody that your father lost his job and is a bum.

SITUATION CARDS (CREATE YOUR OWN)

ACTIVITY SHEET 15

A **GOAL** is something we want to accomplish or get.

We set goals **BEFORE** we act.

Read each sentence below carefully. Decide if the sentence is a **GOAL** or not. Place an X next to the sentences that are **GOALS**.

1. _____ Julie wants to earn an A on her spelling test.

2. _____ Thomas asked his teacher for help.

3. _____ Phil would like to earn extra money to buy his favorite video game.

4. _____ Amy wants to make more friends at school.

5. _____ Melissa invited her friend over for dinner.

6. _____ Mario wants to try out for the baseball team.

7. _____ Martin would like to learn to dive off the high dive board at the pool.

8. _____ Maria helped her mother pick out a gift for her grandmother.

9. _____ Trey wants to go to the movies.

10. _____ Antonia rode the bus home from school.

LESSON 2: AFFECTIVE AND INSTRUMENTAL GOALS

OBJECTIVE

Children will be able to distinguish between *affective* (feeling) goals, *instrumental* (object or activity) goals, and *relationship* (friendship) goals. During this lesson, students will begin to become familiar with taping their responses. Audiotaping and videotaping are integral parts of the latter part of the curriculum. (The material in this lesson may be too advanced for students under age 10. If you are working with a younger group, read over the lesson and decide what content, if any, your group will be able to understand. For example, a group of eight- and nine-year-olds may be able to understand the difference between object and feeling goals. Present the material you think your group can handle.)

Materials

- Tape recorder and blank cassettes
- Flip chart and markers

REVIEW

Review by making a tape of the students as they read situations and goals from the previous session. Allow plenty of time for this review. Although taping the relevant material should take only about five minutes, be prepared for some of the silliness that is bound to occur. Rehearse by going around the group, recording each child telling what she or he had for breakfast that morning or naming a favorite TV show. Play back this tape before proceeding with the review. When you record the students reading situations and goals from the previous session, have them speak slowly and pause for a few seconds between each goal.

ACTIVITIES

1. Play back the tape of students reading (or reviewing) various situations and goals. Before starting the tape, instruct students that you will be asking them to think about the ways goals can be the same and the ways they can be different.

2. After playing the tape, introduce the idea that there are different kinds of goals. The first kind of goal is called *instrumental*, and it involves an *object* or *activity* that someone wants or needs. Provide several examples, such as wanting a new video game, a new stuffed animal, or wanting to go to a movie.

Group Process Tip: Encourage participation by all group members. Be sure to call on quiet members when you're soliciting student ideas during this lesson. Do so in a non-threatening, encouraging manner. Praise students for attempts to contribute. Ask them to praise each other. Also, remind students of group rules, such as no put-downs, and of their agreement to monitor rules.

3. Next, point out that some goals involve wanting (or needing) to be friends with someone else, or wanting to get along with another person. These are *relationship* goals (or friendship goals). Examples would be wanting to be

friends with a new student, or needing to get along better with your brother or sister.

4. Finally, explain that some goals involve wanting to feel a certain way—these are called *affective*, or feeling, goals. Examples would be wanting to feel happy, needing to feel proud of yourself, wanting to stop feeling afraid, or wanting to be satisfied about something.

5. Mention that, often, a feeling goal is closely tied to the other types of goals. For example, "I want to get that new bike, and getting it will make me happy." Still, it is important to think about how they are different ("Being happy is not identical to getting the new bike. There are other things that can make me happy. And getting the new bike won't make me happy forever.").

6. Have students listen to the tape again and label each goal *object/activity*, *feeling*, or *relationship*, or a combination of these. Group leaders can use responses to emphasize the relationships between types of goals.

(Be sure to draw the chart in such a way that you can add another column during the next session.) Notice that many goals involve combinations of feelings, relationships, and activities.

7. At times, students may disagree about whether a goal is affective, on the one

Goal	Type 1. Object/Activity 2. Feeling 3. Relationship	
Martin wants a new bike.	*Object*	
Jasmine needs to feel proud about her schoolwork.	*Feeling*	
Maria wants to go to the mall.	*Activity*	
John would like to get even with Tom.	*Feeling*	
John hopes to be able to stay at Tom's house on Friday night.	*Activity*	
Kristin would like to be friends with Jennifer.	*Relationship*	

hand, or instrumental or relationship, on the other. Encourage them to think of affective goals as ones that are expressed explicitly in terms of a feeling. Remind students that instrumental and relationship goals often have affective goals tied to them.

8. For each instrumental goal and relationship goal, have students give an example of a related affective goal. In order to avoid a sequence of responses such as "A new bike will make me happy," "An ice cream cone will make me happy," and so on, encourage students to think of instrumental or relationship goals they might set in school, such as "wanting to get an A on a test" or "wanting to make friends with a new student." Related affective goals might be, respectively, "hoping to make my parents proud of my grades—that would make me feel proud too" and "wanting to feel like I've helped somebody in a new situation."

9. Keep the chart for use during the next session.

SUMMARIZE THE MAIN IDEA

We can have instrumental (object or activity) goals, relationship (friendship) goals, and affective (feeling) goals. Often an affective goal goes along with the other types of goals, but they are not identical.

Lesson 3: Helpful and Harmful Goals

OBJECTIVE

Children will be able to recognize the difference between *helpful* (prosocial) goals and *harmful* (antisocial) goals.

REVIEW

Materials

- Flip chart from the previous session and markers
- Tape recorder and audiocassettes

Ask students to define the word *goal*. Have someone explain the difference between instrumental, relationship, and affective goals in their own words. Read out loud some of the goals discussed during the previous lesson (or play the tape from the previous session) and, going around the circle, have students identify whether a goal is instrumental, relationship, or affective. Group leaders might also wish to ask whether anyone would like to name a goal they had set since the last session. What type of goal was it?

ACTIVITIES

1. Introduce the idea that there are other ways to think about goals. For example, we can ask whether a goal is helpful or harmful. Examples of helpful goals include
- wanting to make or keep friends
- needing to get along with others
- wanting to do fun things such as going to a movie or a baseball game
- hoping to avoid a fight
- wanting to learn new things

- hoping to get a new book.

In contrast, some harmful goals might be
- wanting to get your way all the time
- needing to be in charge every time
- wanting to tell other people what they should do
- wanting to skip school
- hoping to bring a knife to school.

You can summarize by noting that a goal is helpful when it helps people get along better or when it involves a person getting or keeping something fun or important. A goal is harmful if it makes it harder for people to get along or if it involves getting or keeping something that might hurt someone.

2. Group leaders may wish to remind students about the difference between friendly, neutral, or hostile cues and why it is important to be able to tell the difference among them. The difference between helpful and harmful goals is similar, and it is important to be able to recognize this difference also. This is because when we set goals, we

Group Process Tip: As you elicit students' feedback about helpful and harmful goals, be sure to involve students who are likely to place greater value on helpful (prosocial) goals and behavior, compared to goals that relate to dominating others or simply getting one's way. Directly assist more aggressive group or class members in stating helpful goals and encourage other members to give positive feedback to them. Ask students to comment in a mutually helpful way on one another's opinions about goals. By now the norm or expectation of mutual aid should be established in the group. Encourage members to act on that basis.

are saying, "This is what I want to happen in this situation." The goals we set, in turn, help determine what we choose to do. As upcoming lessons show, helpful goals usually lead to helpful actions and harmful goals usually lead to harmful actions.

3. Using the goals discussed during the previous session, add another column to your chart, showing whether a goal is helpful or harmful. Encourage discussion about why students think a particular goal is helpful or harmful. The chart might look like the one to the right.

4. Notice that, for two of the goals, we placed a question mark in the Helpful or Harmful? column. We think that these goals are probably helpful, but we can think of situations in which they could be harmful. In other words, for each of these goals we need more information before we can decide whether the goal is helpful or harmful. For example, with the goal "to go to the mall," we might want to ask "When? Is it safe to be at the mall? Will there be supervision?"

5. Encourage students to think about what makes a goal helpful or harmful and to be careful not to make a judgment too quickly. Also, encourage them to think of some of the questions they would need to ask before making a judgment. Be a role model and show how self-talk is a good tool for accomplishing this in a situation. Have the students practice using self-talk to

Goal	Type 1. Object/Activity 2. Feeling 3. Relationship	Helpful or Harmful
Martin wants a new bike.	*Object*	*Helpful*
Jasmine needs to feel proud about her schoolwork.	*Feeling*	*Helpful*
Maria wants to go to the mall.	*Activity*	*?*
John would like to get even with Tom.	*Feeling*	*Harmful*
John hopes to be able to stay at Tom's house on Friday night.	*Activity*	*?*
Kristin would like to be friends with Jennifer.	*Relationship*	*Helpful*

think about what makes a goal helpful or harmful. Point out that sometimes a goal might be helpful for one person but harmful for someone else.

6. Discuss with students that, sometimes, a goal might seem helpful at first and turn out later to be harmful. For example, suppose we decide we want to eat an entire bag of chips. Satisfying this goal (eating the chips) might make us feel good now, but in an hour when our mom calls us to dinner, we might get scolded for ruining our appetite, and then we may feel sad. (We might also have a stomachache.)

7. For a homework assignment, ask the students to discuss with parents at least one potential goal for a common social situation.

SUMMARIZE THE MAIN IDEA

Goals can be either helpful or harmful, and it is important to be able to tell the difference.

Note: We have tried to focus on a goal as something a person wants to happen, and to distinguish this from what a person does to reach the goal. As we mentioned in an earlier note, it is not always easy to maintain this distinction. Again, we wish to emphasize the need to increase students' awareness of the difference between what they want, and what they choose to do to make something happen.

Lesson 4: Comparing and Contrasting Goals

OBJECTIVE

To learn about the idea of competing goals, children will be able to compare and contrast goals by answering questions, such as the following:

- Is this an instrumental goal, a relationship goal, or an affective goal?
- Is this a helpful goal or a harmful goal?
- Whom would this goal help? Whom would it hurt?
- How well does the goal fit the situation?

REVIEW

Ask for volunteers to describe the difference between harmful and helpful goals and to distinguish instrumental, relationship, and affective goals. Encourage students to give reasons why they think a particular goal is (a) harmful or helpful and (b) instrumental, relationship, or affective. Remind students that they can use self-talk in real situations when they are trying to make these judgments.

Materials

- Activity sheets 16 to 19 and pencils

ACTIVITIES

1. Explain to students that during this session they will be putting together the concepts they learned during earlier lessons. You will be asking them to write a short script that they will then perform for the group in a role play. (For younger students, group leaders should have a general script prepared and solicit students' input at key points.) You probably won't want to try to record the role plays during this session, but tell the students that you will be videotaping them at the next session.

2. Divide the students into small groups with at least three students to a group. Have students in each group choose a situation about which they would like to write. The situation should be one that students might encounter during or after school, and it should involve two or more students (or a student and an adult) and a problem of some sort (that is, a situation in which something needs to change). Students should write a brief description of the situation, including as many cues as possible. One way to encourage students to generate details is to have them fill out activity sheet 16.

3. Students should clearly identify what needs to change in the situation (or, what one person thinks needs to change). See activity sheet 17.

4. Students should come up with at least

Group Process Tip: Divide students into small groups with care. Pay attention to the strengths and limitations of the students you group together. For example, try to have at least two prosocial students in each small group of four children. Monitor the interactions of the small group closely and intervene if students aren't staying on task or if they are having undue problems with each other.

three possible goals for the situation. Encourage children to generate goals by thinking about what they might want to change in the situation. At this point, they shouldn't think about affective versus instrumental or helpful versus harmful goals.

5. Have students analyze each goal, using activity sheets 18 and 19. When they are finished, encourage them to put together a script for a role play by using their completed activity sheets. The script should involve a "First Person" (the *Making Choices* problem solver), a "Second Person" (the other person, either a peer or an adult, in the situation), and a "Self-Talker," who helps the First Person perform self-talk. It should have four sections, corresponding to the subjects of activity sheets 16 through 19, respectively:

1. What's going on
2. What's the problem (or what needs to change)
3. Possible goals
4. Information about each goal (is it harmful or helpful, for example).

6. Each section of the script should be fairly brief, maybe three or four lines. The Self-Talker can set up the situation, with the other students acting out selected cues. Whenever appropriate, the Self-Talker should encourage the First Person to notice more cues, think about what they mean, think about what should change, and formulate and evaluate possible goals.

7. When a role play has been completed, ask the entire group to evaluate which goal would be best for the situation. Could there be more than one good goal? (Yes!)

8. Introduce the notion of *fit*. Use simple examples, such as how clothes fit or how the pieces of a puzzle fit. Emphasize that when something doesn't fit, it isn't very helpful to us, even though it might be perfectly fine for someone else. For example, we are uncomfortable if we have to wear shoes that don't fit. Explain that another way to think about a goal is whether it fits a specific situation. A particular goal might be fine for one situation, but it might not fit very well in another.

9. Provide a simple example, such as:

You're sitting in the classroom at 2:30 in the afternoon. The teacher announces that she has brought popcorn for everyone. You are really hungry, but you don't like popcorn. You know you have a big candy bar in your bookbag and you wish you could have that instead.

There are several possible goals someone might have in this situation. The first might be to stop being hungry. A second might be to want to eat the candy bar. A third goal might be to wish to get along with the teacher. If school were over and the student were on the playground, the second goal might be fine. However, the first and third goals probably fit this situation—sitting in class at 2:30—better.

10. Encourage students to choose the best possible goal by thinking about how well each fits the particular situation.

11. Conclude by asking students to think about something they would like to change about their behavior in the classroom or at home. Explain that during the next session you will be asking each student to set a personal behavioral goal for school or home. Encourage students to talk with their parents and teachers for help in coming up with a meaningful and attainable goal.

SUMMARIZE THE MAIN IDEA

By using self-talk, and by thinking about what is going on in a situation, we can come up with a variety of potential goals, and we can make judgments about which goals best fit particular situations.

Note: Group leaders may wish to use the activity sheets presented in this lesson during earlier lessons. Activity sheet 18 may be especially helpful in encouraging thinking and discussion about encoding cues.

ACTIVITY SHEET 16

THE SITUATION: *WHAT'S GOING ON?*	What are the cues or clues?	Any other important cues or clues? What are they?	What do the cues or clues mean?
The place...			
The people...			
The time...			
The words...			
The actions...			
The dangers...			
Other...			

ACTIVITY SHEET 17

THE PROBLEM: WHAT NEEDS TO CHANGE?	Who/What EXACTLY?	Why?	Who thinks so? Who doesn't?	Are there more clues or cues?
What somebody is *saying?*				
What somebody is *doing?*				
An object, such as the TV or the radio?				
The place? Is it safe? Is it ____?				
Something else?				

ACTIVITY SHEET 18

GOALS	Goal 1	Goal 2	Goal 3
Describe			
Harmful or helpful?			
Object/activity or relationship?			
Feeling?			
Need more information?			

ACTIVITY SHEET 19

GOAL 1	Harmful: Why or how?	Helpful: Why or how?
First Person _____ (name)		
Peer 1 _____ (name)		
Adult or Peer 2 _____ (name)		

Lesson 5: Setting Personal Goals

OBJECTIVE

Children will increase their ability to demonstrate the skills introduced in the previous lesson. They will also be able to set a personal behavioral goal.

Materials

- Videotape, television, and videocassette recorder
- Scripts from previous lesson
- Flip chart and markers
- Paper and pencils
- Activity sheet 20

REVIEW

Have students describe their role play (or puppet) scripts from the previous lesson. Remind them that you will be videotaping their scenes during this session. Emphasize that today's taping is a chance for them to practice performing while being taped. They will have additional opportunities to write and perform role plays as the *Making Choices* group progresses.

ACTIVITIES

1. Tell students that you will be asking them to set a personal goal at the end of the day's session. While they are performing and observing the role plays, they should be thinking about the steps the actors are going through in figuring out what is going on, what it means, what needs to change, and what goes into choosing goals.

2. Record each group's performance. There will probably be a good deal of silliness and mix-ups, so emphasize to students that this is the first rehearsal. Tell them you expect their best effort during each rehearsal, but that you don't expect perfection and that the rehearsals should be fun.

3. Give students lots of praise and positive feedback for good efforts. Ask them to support and reward each other. Play back the tape, and encourage members to point out when people are using self-talk to find out more about a situation, what it means and what needs to change, and to set goals.

4. Remind students that they will be setting a personal behavioral goal today. Provide some examples of behavioral goals, such as "I want to use my words when I get angry at a peer, not my hands" or "I would like to be able to stop arguing with my teacher (sister, mother, etc.)."

5. Ask each student to name a personal behavioral goal that they would like to set. Group leaders should be receptive to a range of goals, but be careful that goals are meaningful (i.e., they reflect something the student really needs to

Group Process Tip: During this session, students set a personal goal on which they will work at home or in the classroom. Be sure to contact each student's parent and teacher to make sure they understand the process of monitoring goals and that they concur with the goal selected by the student. Ask parents, teachers, or others important in the lives of the children in the group to assist in rewarding students' progress toward their personal goals.

work on) and attainable (i.e., it's realistic that the student can reach, or make good progress towards the goal). Invite students to select a goal that their parents will think is important. (Note: Homework from the previous session will have involved discussion of a goal with a parent or caregiver.) Have students write down their personal goal on a piece of paper.

6. Give each student feedback about his or her proposed goal, and encourage the group to do so by asking questions such as:

Do other students think this would be a good goal for John? Is it important? Is it too easy? Too hard? How will he know whether he's making progress? How will he know when he has reached his goal?

7. Ask students to revise their written goals as needed. When group members are satisfied with their goals, create a chart showing each student's goal, along with a column to show progress. It might look like this:

Note that, in the case of Louis, one can argue that he has set two goals: to finish his work on time and to earn more computer time in class. This may be fine, as long as finishing work means more computer time, consistently. You may want to point out to Louis that his goal has two parts and let him decide whether he wants to revise its phrasing. Changing it to "I would like to finish my work on

Student	Goal	Weekly Progress 0 = no progress 5 = greatest progress					
		Week 1	Week 2	Week 3	Week 4	Week 5	Week 5
James	I want to use words, and not my fists, when I get angry at the kids in class.						
Jasmine	I would like to argue with my sister less often.						
Anna	I would like to do a better job of including my friends in activities.						
Louis	I would like to earn more computer time in class by finishing my work on time.						

time more often" would be a good behavioral goal for the purpose of this group. "I want to earn more computer time during class" would not be.

8. Remind students of the process by which their progress will be monitored. Group leaders should give each child a goal sheet and make sure that each student fills in his or her goal in the appropriate space (see activity sheet 20). Teachers or parents should fill it out every day, noting the student's progress toward the goal. Students should bring their goal sheets in to the next session.

SUMMARIZE THE MAIN IDEA

Today we practiced the steps involved in looking at a situation—figuring out what's going on, what it means, and what needs to change—and in setting goals. We set personal behavioral goals and will be keeping track of our progress over the next weeks.

Note: This lesson requires teacher or parent involvement. Group leaders should contact a parent or teacher of each child before the class to elicit support, to report on progress in the group, and to explain the assignment. Also, for all of the remaining sessions, students should bring in their weekly goal sheets for review. It may prove logistically difficult for students to bring their goal sheets to the sessions and take them back home (or to the school or after-school setting) for daily marking. Use your judgment and work in collaboration with parents and teachers. If you think students will be likely to forget or lose goal sheets, have students keep them at home, in the classroom, or other relevant setting, and ask them to report on their progress. Check in with teachers, parents, and others as well.

ACTIVITY SHEET 20: STUDENT'S PERSONAL GOAL REPORT FORM

Student:	Daily Progress					
Report completed by:	Scoring goals by: 1 = none	2 = limited	3 = OK	4 = good	5 = great	

Goal:

MON	TUE	WED	THU	FRI	SAT	SUN
MON	TUE	WED	THU	FRI	SAT	SUN
MON	TUE	WED	THU	FRI	SAT	SUN
MON	TUE	WED	THU	FRI	SAT	SUN
MON	TUE	WED	THU	FRI	SAT	SUN

Revise or Change Goal?

MON	TUE	WED	THU	FRI	SAT	SUN
MON	TUE	WED	THU	FRI	SAT	SUN
MON	TUE	WED	THU	FRI	SAT	SUN
MON	TUE	WED	THU	FRI	SAT	SUN
MON	TUE	WED	THU	FRI	SAT	SUN

Unit Summary for Group Leaders

In this unit we emphasized that children can learn to think of goals as something they want to obtain or accomplish. A goal can involve an object or activity, a relationship, or a person's feelings. Additionally, goals can be harmful or helpful. Using these ideas, children can learn to think about, compare, and contrast different goals to make a decision about the best goal in a given situation. In this unit we also emphasized that there is a difference between a goal (what a person wants) and what he or she does to reach the goal.

Upon completion of this unit, students should be familiar with the first three steps in *Making Choices* and with the idea that self-talk can help them complete each step more successfully.

They should also be able to formulate a meaningful and attainable personal behavioral goal. To refine these skills, it may be necessary to repeat examples from lessons or even to repeat entire lessons. Before proceeding to unit 5, be sure that students can successfully identify personal goals for a variety of social situations. Give them repeated opportunities to think about different kinds of social situations, about what is going on and what it means, what needs to change, and what they want to happen. The next step in the *Making Choices* program is for children to think about what they can do to reach their goal. That is, they need to *search for and formulate possible responses.*

UNIT 5: RESPONSE SEARCH AND FORMULATION: INVENTING OPTIONS

The fourth step in *Making Choices* is *response search and formulation*. Response search and formulation refers to a child's ability to identify (or, as we call it, invent) multiple potential responses to a social situation or problem. It may involve generating responses from memory (that is, responses that have been used in previous situations), constructing new responses, or both. To interact with others in a prosocial manner and in a variety of social situations, children need to be able to access a wide array of potential responses from which an appropriate one can be chosen.

Research has shown that children who use aggression have difficulty identifying a range of responses in social situations (Rabiner, Lenhart, & Lochman, 1990; Slaby & Guerra, 1988). They conceive only a small number of responses, and they tend to identify responses that rely on coercion and confrontation (Dodge et al., 1995). They are too quick to access heuristics and tend to develop responses that have a poor fit with the situation or problem at hand. The lessons in this unit are designed to help children generate a wider array of responses to social circumstances.

The goal of this unit is to enable children to generate a number of prosocial, nonaggressive potential responses in social situations. There is special emphasis on enabling children to manage and control impulsive behavioral responses through self-talk. At the same time, unit activities are designed to help children increase their repertoires of imaginable responses to confrontational and other social situations.

Lesson 1: Goals and Actions

OBJECTIVE

Children will be able explain the difference between a goal and an action. When presented with a simple social goal, they will demonstrate the ability to generate multiple potential responses (actions).

Materials

- Flip chart and markers
- Activity sheet 21 (lesson enrichment activity)

REVIEW

Begin the review by asking students to report briefly on their progress toward their personal behavioral goals. Have them identify both what they did well and what they need to continue to work on. Emphasize that they will be reporting on their progress at every session. If students are bringing in goal sheets, ask them to turn these in for the first week—be sure to praise those who remembered to bring them, and remember to return the goal sheets to the students before they leave. If students are not bringing in sheets, ask them to remind the group of their goals and to report on their progress. Remind students that they should keep their personal goals in mind during each *Making Choices* session.

Review self-talk with the students and ask for examples of how self-talk can help them figure out what's going on in a situation, what the cues mean, what the problem is, and what someone's goal might be in that situation. Spend ample time with this review to ensure that all students are thoroughly familiar with self-talk. Remind students that an important purpose of the *Making Choices* group is to help them act in ways that are helpful, not harmful, to themselves and others. In the previous unit they learned how to think about and select helpful goals. Emphasize that, in this unit, they will learn to think about different ways they can act to achieve their goals.

ACTIVITIES

1. Introduce the idea that once we have decided on a goal, we need to think about the different actions we might take to achieve that goal. Provide simple examples of the difference between a goal and an action and write them on the flip chart. For example:

2. Ask students to explain the difference between a goal and an action: A goal is something we *want*, an action is something we *do*. You may need to ask questions to elicit this idea from students. It may be helpful to write some version of this statement on a flip chart or blackboard.

Group Process Tip: Emphasize modeling—sharing and demonstrating—in this unit. For example, have students use self-talk to generate a range of responses—"I could try telling my friend that her perfume bothers me, or I could try sitting next to an open window when I'm with her." Ask students who are especially good at self-talk to share their self-talk ideas with other students. Draw out others if need be; encourage students to draw out each other. By now the group should be beyond initial development and members may be able to assume more of the work of the group themselves.

Goals	Actions
To eat something	Go to the cafeteria and eat lunch.
	Ask Mom for a snack.
	Get the granola bar out of your pocket and eat it.
To play a game	Ask your sister if she wants to play.
	Go to the playground and see if other kids are around.
	Call a friend and see if she can come over.

3. Explain to students that we can usually think of more than one action we might take to reach a goal. Ask them for more examples of things they might do to reach the goals just discussed. Have students name several other simple goals and generate possible actions to reach them. Point out that we must usually complete more than one action in order to reach a goal.

4. For young students, introduce the concept of *imagination* and ask if anyone can define the word. For older students, steer the discussion toward a definition such as, "We can use our imagination to think of all the things that we might do. They can be real or make-believe." Introduce the related idea: "Our imaginations can also help us think of ways to act that we had never thought of before."

5. Acknowledge that we often use our imaginations to think about make-believe ideas and to daydream, but that we can also use our imaginations to think of new and creative ways to act. Point out that using our imaginations is one way we can stop and think. When we're in a difficult situation, we can use our imaginations to think of a good way to reach a goal. Emphasize to older students that use of imagination can lead to new and creative ideas about how to act in social situations. Point out that we can use self-talk to unlock our imaginations, that is, push our minds to invent new and creative things.

6. Model lots of examples of self-talk, and have students do so as well.

SUMMARIZE THE MAIN IDEA

A goal is something we want to have or accomplish. An action is something we do to reach a goal. We can usually think of, or imagine, many different actions that might help us reach a goal.

LESSON ENRICHMENT ACTIVITIES

1. Have students draw a picture illustrating two things they might do to reach a specific goal. Be sure they clearly state and label the goal and that they label each action separately. Students can use goals discussed during the lesson or come up with new ones.

2. Have students complete activity sheet 21.

ACTIVITY SHEET 21: GENERATING RESPONSES

FOR EACH GOAL, WRITE AT LEAST THREE THINGS YOU MIGHT DO TO REACH THAT GOAL.

GOAL	RESPONSES
I want to be friends with the new student.	1. 2. 3.
I want to make good grades.	1. 2. 3.
I want to have enough money to buy a CD.	1. 2. 3.
I want to get along better with my brother.	1. 2. 3.

Lesson 2: Feelings and Actions

OBJECTIVE

Students will be able to provide examples of how feelings can influence actions. They will also be able to describe strategies that will help them stop and think before they act when they are experiencing strong and difficult feelings.

Materials

- Flip chart and markers
- Staircase diagram of *Making Choices* steps 1 to 4

REVIEW

Check in with students about their progress on their personal goals and collect goal sheets (if applicable). Encourage students to use the *Making Choices* skills they are learning, especially self-talk, to work on their goals.

Review briefly the difference between a goal and an action. Ask students to think back to unit 1 and the different feelings that people can have. Have students give examples of the basic feelings and of the situations that might lead to each. Remind them that people experience different degrees of feelings—for example, someone can be a little angry or very angry.

ACTIVITIES

1. Explain to students that you will be talking about how a person's feelings can influence his or her actions. Begin by making sure everyone understands the difference between a feeling (or how we feel) and an action (or what we do). Emphasize that we sometimes use actions to express a feeling.

2. Provide several examples of when a feeling might lead directly to an action. Ask students for their ideas. Examples might be:

- When Anna suddenly felt very happy, she jumped up and down and yelled.
- When she was feeling sad, Jasmine left the room.
- When Jonathan got very angry, he threw his book on the floor.

3. Ask students to think of feelings such as anger, sadness, or frustration. With students' help, talk about situations that might lead to each.

4. Have students think about a situation that might make them angry. For example, they might think about a time when someone broke a favorite toy or did something to hurt them. Point out to students that sometimes when we are experiencing a strong and difficult feeling, it can make us forget to stop and think before we act. Strong feelings can make us forget to notice and pay attention to all the cues in a situation, to think of what

Group Process Tip: During this session, you will be asking students to imagine a time when they were angry or sad. This is a routine exercise, but it occasionally elicits negative feelings. Watch that students don't act these feelings out with each other in a destructive way. Help members move back out of "remembering" and into the present. For example, have them close their eyes and take the time to "fly" (or "morph," etc.) out of the past and into the present, where they have new skills they have learned in the group.

the cues might mean, to figure out what needs to change, and to think of helpful goals. Finally, it can make us forget to imagine all the possible things we might be able to do in the situation. (Group leaders may wish to present this idea with the staircase diagram found at the end of the manual.)

5. Explain to students that whenever we are experiencing a strong and difficult emotion, that's the most important time to remember to use *Making Choices* skills ("stop-and-think" skills). Encourage students to remember how to tell when they are becoming angry (ask what the cues are or where they "feel" anger in their bodies). When they notice some of these anger cues, it's time to use self-talk to turn on their stop-and-think skills.

6. Use physical gestures and simple slogans to emphasize this message. For example, select a student to describe where, in her body, she first feels anger. Suppose it's in her stomach. Ask her to pretend she is getting angry and then to practice a set of simple steps to help her remember the stop-and-think skills. The steps might be as follows:
- I feel anger in my stomach.
- I need to touch my stomach with one hand and gently pat it.
- I need to count to ten while I'm patting my stomach.
- I need to stop, think, and pay attention to what's going on.

Group leaders should encourage the other students to practice these steps. With young children, you can act out these actions with them, exaggerating the motions and movements. Sometimes it can be fun and effective to make up a simple song, rhyme or slogan, or pantomime that will help children remember steps such as these.

7. Emphasize that doing things like counting to ten or taking deep breaths can prevent us from acting too quickly when we are very angry or frustrated. Most of the time, this will help us stop and think of new and creative ways to behave. Unless we stop and think, we are likely to act impulsively, based on our anger or frustration. That's when somebody is likely to get hurt and when we are likely to get in trouble.

SUMMARIZE THE MAIN IDEA

Feelings, especially strong and difficult feelings, can make us forget to stop and think before we act. However, we can often learn ways that help us turn on our *Making Choices* skills.

LESSON ENRICHMENT ACTIVITY

Practice counting to ten, taking deep breaths, and other "slow-down" exercises. Generate some simple slogans and pantomimes that might help children remember to use one or more exercises. You can have the group as a whole complete this activity or use smaller subgroups.

Lesson 3: Using Self-Talk to Generate Responses

OBJECTIVE

Students will increase their ability to use self-talk to generate multiple potential responses in a difficult situation.

REVIEW

Discuss with students their progress toward their personal goals and, if applicable, collect goal sheets.

Materials

- Conflict situation cards (you can use the cards from unit 1 or create new ones)
- Activity sheets 16 to 19 and 22
- Video camera and tapes
- Flip chart and markers

Present a simple situation for the students, describing the main cues and their meanings, and formulate a goal. For example:

Suppose you're walking to the cafeteria before school. You're trying to get to the cafeteria before breakfast is over because you're hungry, and you don't have much time. You see your best friend by his locker and he calls you over. He is eating cookies in the hall, which is against the rules. He asks you if you want one. You look around and see there are no other kids or teachers in sight. You think for a minute, then decide on a goal: You want to eat something but you want to stay out of trouble. What could you do?

Go around the circle or class and ask students for possible actions. Encourage as many responses as possible. Then tell students,

Imagine you see your friend standing at your locker, eating your cookies (which you were saving for after school). How would that make you feel? Would it lead you to come up with different responses?

Remind students that in this type of situation it is important to remember to stop and think before taking an action. Ask students to name some strategies that could help them stop and think.

ACTIVITIES

1. Tell students that you will be videotaping them as they perform role plays (or puppet shows) that demonstrate *Making Choices* skills. Emphasize again that this is a rehearsal and that, although you expect them to do their best, the performance does not have to be perfect.

2. Divide the students into groups of two. Give each pair of students a situation card and ask each pair to study the card. Encourage the students to talk with their partners about the situation. Have them write down (or, for younger

Group Process Tip: This activity involves pairing students and having them brainstorm potential responses. Use your insight into the strengths and limitations of students when you create pairs—make sure you don't put together two students who will build on each other's negative behavior. And be sure to monitor and guide the brainstorming. The note about brainstorming at the end of the lesson reviews guidelines for planning and conducting this activity.

students, draw pictures of) a self-talk script to describe briefly the situation, the cues and what they mean, what needs to change, potential goals, and the best goal. Remind students about the need to generate helpful rather than harmful goals. (You may wish to have students use activity sheets 16 to 19 in writing their scripts.) Using the chosen situation, have students complete activity sheet 22 to stimulate response search and formulation. The scripts can be brief, with one- or two-sentence descriptions or pictures of each of the first three problem-solving steps. Students should focus on generating at least three or four responses in their scripts.

3. Have each pair of students rehearse their script. Group leaders should rotate among the groups to ensure good participation. After about 10 minutes of rehearsals, videotape each pair of students performing a script. Play it back and comment on the performances, pointing out when students used self-talk to accomplish one or more *Making Choices* skills. It is especially important to point out and praise students' efforts to generate multiple responses.

Note: In the next unit, we describe strategies for evaluating responses (whether they are helpful or harmful, how well they fit a situation and goal, and so on). The emphasis in this unit has been to encourage children to generate multiple responses. Generally, the more responses the better, so encourage students to be creative and

imaginative. It may be necessary, however, to place limits on what is and is not an acceptable response. For example, unlikely and even imaginary responses ("I would give the mean boy a magic pill so he will be nice," for example) are okay during this Making Choices *step, as long as they are at least somewhat related to the situation at hand. Coming up with silly and imaginative responses can be fun and may enhance the creative process, so let the kids' imaginations flow. At the same time, group leaders will want to keep things from getting too silly. You can laugh with students and come up with some unlikely responses yourself, but be sure not to spend more than a couple of minutes before redirecting the discussion to more serious responses.*

Another potential problem is when students generate aggressive and violent responses. As we mentioned in the introduction to this book, our approach is to enable children to see that they have behavioral choices. In real life, group members are likely to think of aggression as a possible response when confronted with a situation they don't like. For some children, this may be the only type of response they can think of. It is important that students be able to acknowledge thoughts such as, "If Louis doesn't stop bothering me, I'm going to hit him."

Children can learn to avoid responding with an impulsive aggressive action by practicing skills related to the six steps of Making Choices. *One of these skills involves thinking about all the things they might do—including the use of aggression. Making Choices skills can equip children with the ability to think about aggression as one potential response—and to move beyond it—to create alternative responses that rely on negotiation, compromise, and other relationship-enhancing strategies. To understand and acquire this skill, children must practice each problem-solving step, including the step where they consider using aggression.*

In allowing children to explore aggressive responses, place limits on the language that is used and make sure that plenty of other more positive responses are given. For example, group leaders might decide it is okay for group members to say something such as, "In this situation I would want to hit Louis." They should, on the other hand, make clear that prolonged and graphic descriptions of a violent response are not acceptable during the Making Choices group. If, when redirected, a child persists in suggesting responses that refer to sexual assault, serious physical assaults, and other severe forms of aggression, group leaders must put an immediate end to brainstorming by that student. They should also consult with parents, teachers, school counselors, or mental health clinicians to determine whether that student's continued participation in the group is desired or whether a different intervention is indicated.

SUMMARIZE THE MAIN IDEA

When we have chosen a goal for a situation, we then have to figure out what to do to reach the goal. We can usually think of many possible things we might do to reach our goals. It is a good idea to do this so that we can choose the best action to take to reach our goal.

ACTIVITY SHEET 22

ALTERNATIVE SOLUTIONS

For each situation described, write or draw two or three alternative responses.

1. During a soccer game you lose control of the ball to a player on the other team. You get angry.

What can you do?

What else can you do?

What else can you do?

ACTIVITY SHEET 22

ALTERNATIVE SOLUTIONS

For each situation described, write or draw two or three alternative responses.

2. You ask your mom if you can sleep over at a friend's house. She says yes, if you can finish all your chores and your homework. You know you will need help; you decide you want your sister to help you, but you think she may still be mad at you because you yelled at her last night.

What can you do?

What else can you do?

What else can you do?

ACTIVITY SHEET 22

ALTERNATIVE SOLUTIONS
For each situation described, write or draw two or three alternative responses.

3. While practicing writing, you make a mistake and the paper is ruined. You decide you need a break, but you know you have lots and lots of homework to do.

What can you do?

What else can you do?

What else can you do?

Unit Summary for Group Leaders

In this unit students have learned to use self-talk to invent multiple potential responses in social situations. We have emphasized the need to encourage children to think about and imagine all the possible things they might do to reach their goals in a situation. Potential responses might include the use of aggression, and at this step in *Making Choices* it is okay to think of aggression as one possible response. The emphasis in this unit is on generating numerous alternatives so that students recognize that they have behavioral choices.

Group leaders have also provided children with many opportunities to practice the *Making Choices* steps that lead up to response search and formulation. Students have begun also to apply *Making Choices* skills in other settings, and they are discussing their progress on personal behavioral goals as part of each session's review.

During the next step of *Making Choices*, *response decision*, students will learn to evaluate the numerous possible responses they have generated. From these, they will learn to select the best response to reach their goals.

UNIT 6: RESPONSE DECISION: MAKING A CHOICE

The fifth step in *Making Choices* is *response decision*, the point at which a child reviews all potential response alternatives, evaluating each on several dimensions, such as the likely outcomes of the response and the degree of confidence the child has that he or she is capable of carrying out the response. This evaluation leads to the selection of one or more specific responses for enactment. It involves making a choice.

Research suggests that aggressive children are more likely than other children to select aggressive responses over prosocial responses (Slaby & Guerra, 1988).

The goal of this unit is for children to learn to select prosocial, nonaggressive responses in social situations.

Children who are aggressive often misjudge the consequences (or outcomes) of aggressive actions. For example, aggressive children often believe that aggressive responses will result in positive—that is, desired—outcomes.

They also have greater confidence in their ability to carry out aggressive responses, compared with responses that depend on prosocial skills such as negotiating or compromising (Perry, Perry, & Rasmussen, 1986). Additionally, compared with other children, aggressive children tend to evaluate the content of coercive and aggressive responses more favorably—believing, for example, "hitting is okay" (Guerra et al., 1995).

Lesson 1: Responses and Their Outcomes

OBJECTIVE

Children will be able to define *outcome* (in developmentally appropriate language) and name several likely outcomes of a particular response.

REVIEW

Check with students on progress toward their personal behavioral goals. Ask them to evaluate whether they have achieved the goal or whether the goal needs to be modified. Remind them to use *Making Choices* skills to reach their goals. Be sure to praise compliance with the goal sheet system.

Review briefly the four steps of problem solving discussed to date. Ask students to explain how feelings can influence each step. Use the staircase diagram to remind students of the steps, and ask them to give examples of how self-talk can help at each step. Carry the discussion about *Making Choices* skills to the point at which a person has generated a number of potential responses.

ACTIVITIES

1. Explain to students that during this session they are going to learn to evaluate (or judge) the potential responses they have generated, in order to choose the best response. During the next several sessions, you will be talking about a number of ways to evaluate a response. The first will be to judge an action (or response) in terms of its likely outcomes.

2. Introduce the idea that whenever we are in a situation and take an action, something about the situation changes. Give some simple examples, such as,

- You come into a room that is stuffy and hot. You take an action: You open the window. This action changes something about the room. It lets air in and the room gets cooler.
- Antonia is playing outside and is getting cold. She takes an action: She puts on her jacket. This action changes something about the situation. Antonia is warmer.
- Louis is playing with a puzzle and is getting bored. He takes an action: He walks to where James is building a tower with blocks and knocks over

Materials

- Staircase diagram
- Flip chart and markers
- Dominoes

Group Process Tip: Take stock of group development. By this time group members may be settled into a comfortable way of doing things. Assess whether this is so, and if it is, whether this serves to promote group goals and member relationships. Are the roles and norms that have evolved helpful? If the group has not developed, determine why and what might be done. Take another look at the material on group process and development in the introduction and remain an active facilitator, even if things are going well. At the same time, encourage group members to take responsibility for group activities.

the tower. This action changes something about James. James gets angry.

3. Explain to students that when something changes in a situation, we call this an outcome. In these examples, "James gets angry," "Sadie is warmer," and "It lets air in and the room gets cooler" are outcomes. We can use this idea to define outcome; for example: An outcome of an action or response is anything that changes because of the action or response. A response can have more than one outcome, and most responses have many outcomes.

4. Another way to think of an outcome is to ask what happens next. For example, what happened next when Louis knocked over the tower? (James got mad.) Thinking of outcomes in this way helps us realize that an action can lead to a chain of events (a sequence of outcomes) and that it is important to consider all the possible outcomes of a response when we are trying to judge it. To return to James and Louis, what happens next when James gets angry? He might cry, he might tell the teacher, or he might hit Louis. These are possible outcomes of Louis's initial action, knocking over the tower.

5. We can talk about short-term and long-term outcomes. When we ask what will change we are usually asking about short-term outcomes, that is, what in the situation will change immediately

because of a response? Asking what happens next can help us think about long-term outcomes.

6. Most older children will be familiar with a concept that is closely related to our definition of outcomes: Every action has consequences.

7. Create a chart showing several simple responses, along with short- and long-term outcomes. Encourage students to generate as many of both kinds of outcomes as possible. They can use self-talk to ask about each response, asking what will change and what happens next. The chart might look something like the one on page 147.

You may need to help younger students generate outcomes. Encourage older students to generate meaningful responses and outcomes themselves.

SUMMARIZE THE MAIN IDEA

Every response has one or more outcomes. One way to judge a response is to think about its likely outcomes.

LESSON ENRICHMENT ACTIVITY

Illustrate the idea that an action can trigger a sequence of outcomes by setting up a row of dominoes. Tip over the first domino and watch as the entire row tumbles. Point out that knocking over the first domino is an action that causes multiple outcomes.

Response or action	What will change?	What happens next?	What happens next?	What happens next?
Antonia puts on her jacket.	She gets warmer.	She stays outside a little longer.	Some kids ask her to join them.	Antonia has a great afternoon.
Louis knocks down the block tower.	James gets angry.	James tells the teacher what Louis did.	Louis has to take a time out.	James uses the blocks, then reads a book.
Tom asks John to play checkers.	John becomes less angry.	They play checkers.	Tom shares his snack with John.	They play ball after school.
Anna goes on a trip with her family. She brings home a gift for her new neighbor Tonya.	Tonya is thrilled.	Anna and Tonya play together.	Tonya invites Anna for a sleep-over.	Anna and Tonya become good friends.

Lesson 2: Harmful and Helpful Outcomes

OBJECTIVE

Students will be able to distinguish harmful outcomes from helpful ones to judge various responses to a social situation.

Materials

- Flip chart and markers
- Chart from previous session
- Activity sheet 23

REVIEW

Check with students on progress toward their personal behavioral goals. Ask for examples of how they used problem solving to work toward their goals. Review and modify goals as needed.

Display the chart created during the previous session. Ask for volunteers to describe the outcomes of a particular response. Remind students that they can use self-talk to ask about a response: "What will change?" and "What will happen next?"

ACTIVITIES

1. Ask students to think back to the unit on goals and how they learned to decide whether a goal is helpful or harmful. Today you will be asking them to look at a particular response (and its likely outcomes) and to decide whether it is helpful or harmful. Emphasize that this is one of the most important things to consider when judging a response. Explain also that, for a particular response, it is important to look at each outcome separately and judge whether the outcome is harmful or helpful. Mention to older students that some responses might have both helpful and harmful outcomes.

2. Ask students to recall activity sheets 18 and 19, which they used to help them decide whether a goal was helpful or harmful. Explain that you will be filling out a similar sheet, on the flip chart, to help them judge whether the outcomes of a response are helpful or harmful. The chart might look something like activity sheet 23.

3. Have students generate common social situations and complete the first four steps of *Making Choices*. Once you have a list of potential responses, write at least three of them on the chart. (You may wish to use situations the group has discussed previously. If you do so, it is still a good idea to briefly go through the steps again to help students remember and practice *Making Choices* skills.) Lead a group discussion to generate potential outcomes for each response. For each outcome, solicit input from the students to complete the chart.

Group Process Tip: This lesson uses self-talk to help students think about the potential outcomes of their actions. Be sure to model self-talk over and over again for students. Have students demonstrate self-talk. Help students who are having trouble doing self-talk in a productive and prosocial way. Encourage all students to give positive feedback to each other, even for small steps.

4. Remind students that the "First Person" refers to the person who performs an action or a response and the "Second Person" is someone else who is present in the situation (a peer or a teacher, for example). When students are thinking about whether an outcome is harmful or helpful, they need to think about how it will affect all the people in a situation. The chart you create can have columns for a Third and a Fourth Person.

5. When trying to judge whether an outcome is helpful, students can use self-talk to ask themselves questions about whether the outcome is helpful for each person in the situation. You should demonstrate self-talk, especially for younger students. Be sure to include questions about yourself and others in the situation. For example:

- How will the outcome make me feel? How will it make Jasmine feel?
- Will the outcome make something better for me? Will it make something better for Louis?
- Will the outcome help me get along with Antonia? Will it help Susan get along with Antonia?
- Will I like the outcome? Will Thomas like the outcome? How about John?
- Will the outcome make me get something I want? Will it make Juan get something he wants?
- Will the outcome make me learn something new? Will it help my sister learn something new?

- Will the outcome make me keep something I need? Will it make the new kid keep something he needs?

6. Students can also use self-talk to ask similar questions to judge whether an outcome is harmful for themselves and others in a situation:

- Will the outcome make something worse for me? Will it make something worse for Alex?
- How will the outcome make me feel? How will it make Anna feel?
- Would I like the outcome if I were John? Would I like it if I were Thomas?
- Will the outcome make it harder for me to get along with my brother? Will it make it harder for my brother to get along with me?
- Will the outcome make me lose something that I like? Will it make Antonia lose something she likes?
- Will the outcome prevent me from getting something I want? Will it prevent Juan from getting something he wants? How about Thomas?

7. Remind students that if they are experiencing a strong and difficult emotion in a situation, it may not be easy to stop and think about outcomes. Emphasize that it is especially important to remember to do so in such situations. Remind them of any slogans, songs, or pantomimes from the previous unit that will help them stop and think. They might also try to remember to take a series of deep breaths or to count to ten.

8. For older students, explain again that the responses they are judging can have both harmful and helpful outcomes. Emphasize that it is important to be able to make an overall judgment about each potential response. Unfortunately, no formula—"A response with one very harmful outcome for one person and two very helpful outcomes for three people is better than a response with no harmful outcomes but a moderately helpful outcome for one person," for example—exists for weighing one response or outcome against another. Ask students how they would compare several responses, each with a mix of helpful and harmful outcomes.

9. Emphasize to all students the need to pay close attention to responses that have any harmful outcomes. Whenever they judge a potential response to have even a single harmful outcome, they should recognize this as a signal that they need to stop and think some more, before they act. They may need to look at and judge additional responses, or they may need to move back to an earlier step of *Making Choices*. For example, if they looked at all the possible responses in a situation, and every one had at least one harmful outcome, then they either need more information (that is, they need to look for more clues or to give more thought to the meaning of the cues), they need to formulate a different goal ("I want something different than I thought"), or they need to generate additional responses ("What else could I do?").

10. It is important for group leaders and students to begin thinking about "putting it all together," that is, summarizing the main ideas they have learned. Therefore, remind students that there will be four or five more sessions, and ask them to be thinking about what they have learned and how they can use *Making Choices* skills. Explain that they will be putting together a videotaped role play (puppet show or other comparable activity) that will demonstrate the six steps in *Making Choices*. Remind students that they have already written and rehearsed role plays dealing with the first four steps, and that they may choose to continue with existing scripts or begin a new one. During the next couple of sessions they will begin writing a script dealing with the fifth step. We recommend that group leaders and students plan to host a performance of the video (or puppet show) for teachers and family members during the very last session. If you choose to do so, tell students that the group will need to begin planning for this during an upcoming session.

SUMMARIZE THE MAIN IDEA

One important way to judge a response is to decide whether it is helpful or harmful. To do this, we need to think about each likely outcome of the response and whether it will help or harm the people in a situation.

ACTIVITY SHEET 23

Response or Action:				
	First Person (ME)		**Second Person**	
	Helpful?	Harmful?	Helpful?	Harmful?
What changes?				
What happens next?				
What happens next?				

Lesson 3: Confidence and Response Decision

OBJECTIVE

Students will be able to define *confidence* and to name one or two problem-solving skills at which they are good and which they might use in a problematic social situation.

Note: Some of the concepts presented in this lesson may be too complex for students below the third or fourth grade. Adapt the lesson to fit the developmental level of your group members.

Materials

- Flip chart and markers
- Activity sheets 16 to 19, and 22 to 24
- Pencils

REVIEW

Check with students about progress on their behavioral goals. Students who have made good progress on a goal in one area (school, for example) may wish to develop a goal for a different area.

Go around the circle and ask students for examples from the previous week of responses, outcomes, and whether the outcomes were helpful or harmful. Prompt them with the chart you created, if needed.

ACTIVITIES

1. Introduce the concept of confidence. For young children, the story about *The Little Engine that Could* is a good way to talk about confidence—"I think I can, I know I can." Come up with a definition, and write it on the flip chart, that emphasizes the notion that being confident means feeling that "I can do this!"

2. Explain that in order to feel confident, not only must we feel that we can do something but we must also believe that the "something"—whatever it is—will help us reach our goals.

3. Remind students that one purpose of *Making Choices* is to help them become more effective and confident in social situations. The exercises and games they have completed so far were designed to help them build new social skills (that is, the first component of confidence). With continued practice their abilities will increase. Group leaders should point out the skills that students have mastered, being sure to praise the progress each student has made.

Group Process Tip: Students are asked to identify and describe each other's problem-solving skills and strengths during this lesson. Actively demonstrate this for students, and encourage them to talk about and reinforce each other's skills. If students are having a hard time identifying the problem-solving skills of their peers, have them begin with more basic social skills (for example, "Juan is very friendly," or "Jasmine helped me yesterday"). Provide lots of praise for students' efforts.

4. Ask students to name one or two new *Making Choices* skills they have learned. Also, ask students to describe a peer's new skills (for example, you might say, "Alan, give me an example of one *Making Choices* skill that Anna can do

well"). Provide lots of coaching and modeling to help students describe their own and peers' skills.

5. Emphasize again that to feel confident about a response students must also believe that the response will work, that it will get them what they want or need. Provide some simple examples, such as:

- I know I can make the teacher hear me if I yell in class. But I'm not confident that yelling will get me some time on the computer. It just wouldn't do any good.
- I know I can run fast on the playground. But I'm not confident I could beat John in a race. He's two years older and much bigger and faster. No matter how fast I can run, I won't beat him this year.

6. Note that sometimes a response won't work because it's just not good enough—running fast, for example—but that other times it doesn't work because the response doesn't fit the situation—if you yell in class the teacher will probably hear you, but it probably won't get you what you want, because yelling doesn't belong in the classroom. Emphasize that there is something students can do build their confidence for both kinds of responses.

7. Responses can be strong or weak (bigger, faster, better, and so on). Emphasize that students can practice and work harder to increase their skills, which will increase the chances that a response will be effective. Point out that even when we know we are good at something, we can improve.

8. Discuss the concept of practice. Ask whether students think that Michael Jordan (basketball), Monica Seles (tennis), Michael Johnson (track), or local heroes practice. Note that some responses do not work even with practice (even Jordon has lost basketball games).

9. Explain that when we believe a response will not work because it doesn't fit the situation, this is a signal that we need to stop and get more information. Perhaps we need to look at the other potential responses we generated. Maybe we need to go back and generate additional responses. Or maybe we need to go to one of the earlier *Making Choices* steps. But first we need to be sure to use self-talk and ask ourselves why the response doesn't fit the situation. For example:

- Is it the wrong time or place for the response? Yelling is okay on the playground but maybe not in class?
- Does the response deal with the problem? Will the response change the things I think need to change in the situation?
- Will the response help me reach my goal for the situation—will the response produce the kind of change I want to happen?
- Is the response too strong for the situation—it might work, but it might

also be too difficult to enact, and it might have outcomes I can't think of?

- Am I just too angry or frustrated to perform the response the right way?

Answering questions such as these should help us generate new and different responses (or modify the current response) to fit the situation better. When we believe a response fits a situation well, we have greater confidence that the response will work.

10. Split the group into groups of two or three students each and ask them to use activity sheets 16 to 19, 22, and 23 to write a script demonstrating how to evaluate multiple responses (that is, how to decide which response is best). Have each group use a situation from a previous role play that had been carried as far as step 4 (response search). Spend a few minutes talking about the situation with each group to be sure everyone understands it. Group leaders may wish to review the first four problem-solving steps briefly and to suggest no more than three potential responses for the students to evaluate. Encourage students to use self-talk when they are working on the activity sheets.

11. Before closing, bring the students together and ask each student to name a *Making Choices* skill they can perform well. Which skills do they think are especially important or effective? Why?

SUMMARIZE THE MAIN IDEA

We feel confident about a response when we believe that we have the ability to perform the response and when we believe the response will help us reach our goals.

LESSON ENRICHMENT ACTIVITY

Use activity sheet 24 to have students identify two or three things they can do well. Encourage them to identify at least one skill they have learned in the *Making Choices* group.

ACTIVITY SHEET 24

CONFIDENCE

I AM GOOD AT:

_____

_____

_____

_____

_____

_____

_____

_____

_____

_____

_____

_____

_____

_____

Lesson 4: Choosing a Response

OBJECTIVE

Students will be able to evaluate multiple potential responses and to choose one appropriate response for enactment. They will be able to state several reasons for their choices.

Materials

- Flip chart and markers
- Activity sheet 25 (older students) or 26 (younger students)
- Pencils
- One set of number cards (1-10) for each student
- Tally sheet

Note: You will probably need two sessions to cover this material adequately. One strategy would be to introduce the new material and complete the activities with the entire group during one session. During a second session have students break down into groups to repeat the activities so they can continue to develop role play scripts.

REVIEW

Check with students about progress on their behavioral goals.

Ask students to name a *Making Choices* skill in which they are confident. Review the two components of confidence—skills, plus the belief that a response will help you reach your goal—and the things people can do to increase their confidence in a response. Review the other ways we can judge a response—that is, by its likely outcomes and by whether it is harmful or helpful.

Emphasize to students that now it is time to perform a critical step in *Making Choices*: It's time to choose the best response—to make a choice.

Remind students that they will be continuing with their role play scripts today.

ACTIVITIES

1. Choose one of the situations being used by a group for their role play. Using the appropriate activity sheets from previous lessons, guide students through the first four steps of problem solving for the situation. Once a list of potential responses has been generated, ask students to judge each by

- identifying its likely outcomes
- deciding whether it is harmful or helpful
- evaluating their own confidence that they can perform the response and that the response will get them what they want or need.

Group Process Tip: This lesson involves consolidation of old and new material. Be sure to repeat concepts from previous lessons and to link them with the material in this lesson. Link them also with group goals. Listen for feedback from your group suggesting that (a) they know the old material and are bored with repetition, or that (b) they have not mastered the old material and need more practice. Also, note that the ending phase of the group is approaching. Anticipate how students are going to deal with ending and how you can help ensure that they retain—and will use—what they've learned.

2. Emphasize that it is now time to choose one response from the possible alternatives.

3. Explain that one way to make a decision when you have to choose one item (response) from several alternatives is to give each item a score, and then choose the one with the highest score. Give several simple examples:

- Jasmine says she likes *Barney* this much (hold hands a foot apart) and she likes *Sesame Street* this much (hold hands a yard apart). She chooses to watch *Sesame Street*.
- Louis can have either cake or ice cream. On a scale of 1 to 10, he would give ice cream a 9 and cake a 7. He chooses ice cream.
- Anna gives the movie with Brad Pitt five stars. The movie with Leonardo DiCaprio gets two stars. She chooses to go see the Brad Pitt movie.

Use examples with other current movies, CDs, video games, and so on.

4. Older children will probably understand this concept readily and be able to give numerous examples. For younger children, stick with simple visual descriptors for "how much."

5. Tell students that when it's time to choose a response, they can think of themselves as "the judge," whose job it is to consider all the responses and give

each a score. For older children, mention an example that they might see on television:

Suppose you're watching a diving competition or figure skating on TV. Usually there will be a group of four or five judges. Each contestant takes a turn, and then the judges give him or her a score from one to ten. These numbers are added together and the contestant with the highest score wins.

Just like the judges in the sports contests, students will now have to look at each response and give it a score.

6. Ask older students to imagine that the responses they have generated for a situation are like the contestants in a diving match. Give each student a set of number cards, 1 to 10. Read out the situation you have been discussing and summarize each potential response and how you have evaluated it so far. Then repeat each response slowly. After each response, have students hold up a number to show how they would score the response. Tally up the numbers, noting the score each student gave. For each response, ask each student why he or she chose that score. (The first time you do this exercise, limit responses to two.)

7. As mentioned in the previous lesson, there is no single formula for assigning scores to a response. We can, however, offer some guidelines (see activity sheets 25 and 26). Let older students use activity sheet 25 as a guide for

assigning scores, and complete the previous exercise again.

8. With younger students, use a simple scoring system for responses, perhaps consisting of stars (0 stars = poor, 1 star = good, 2 stars = excellent). Activity sheet 26 provides an example. Group leaders can devise scoring sheets that lie somewhere between the two provided, depending on the age and developmental level of group members.

9. To help younger children practice scoring different responses, you can use familiar children's stories, such as *Little Red Riding Hood* or *Jack and the Beanstalk*. In the first story, ask students to pretend for a moment that they are Little Red Riding Hood, and that they want to go see their grandmother, who lives in the forest. What could they do? Possible responses might be to:

- walk alone through the forest to Grandma's
- ask a friend to go along.

Ask students to use activity sheet 26 to score both of these responses. Which would be best? You can complete a similar exercise for Jack. For example, when he needed money and the beans were offered in exchange for his cow, what could he have done?

10. Emphasize that when a response receives an "excellent" score, it is probably the one to choose. If more than one receives a score of excellent,

look at each again to determine which is better. If none of the potential responses receives a score of excellent, students should stop and think and go back to an earlier step of *Making Choices*. They can use the score to help them decide how far back they need to go. For example, if no potential response receives a score higher than "poor," students would need to go back at least to the response formulation step and come up with additional alternatives. If one or more responses are "good," students may be able to modify one and rescore. Encourage students not to choose a response until they find one that is "excellent."

11. Explain to students that one important way to get more information about a response is to ask yourself how it will make you feel after you have performed it. Will it make you feel proud of yourself? Another useful way to judge a response is to think of a person you respect, such as a parent, older brother or sister, aunt or uncle, teacher, and so on. Think about how that person would feel if he or she found out you had performed the response. Would they be proud of you? If the answer is no, then even a response that received a 10 would not be a good choice. This can be a helpful final check for the response you have chosen.

12. Emphasize to students that they can also evaluate a potential response by thinking how much it is like—or

different from—previous responses they have tried either in the current situation or in earlier situations. If the response is just like a response they tried earlier, it would be a good idea to ask questions such as "Did it work before?" "Why or why not?" "Was it helpful or harmful?" "How do I know?" "Has the situation changed since I tried this?" "How?" "Why might the response work this time if it didn't work before?" When students are writing scripts for their role plays (or puppet show), have them stop the action at this point in the problem-solving sequence so the narrator can ask these questions.

13. Have students finish the script for today's role play. Although you won't be taping it, encourage them to do their best. Emphasize that the role play today should focus on how students evaluate two or more alternative responses to choose the best one for enactment.

14. Have the groups perform their role plays. Be sure to praise students' efforts and offer constructive feedback where needed (for example, "Alan, I really liked the way you helped the others figure out how to use the scoring sheets today. But I don't think I understood why you gave the first response a score of 10. Maybe you can be thinking of your reasons over the next couple of days and help us understand it better next time.").

SUMMARIZE THE MAIN IDEA

Once we have identified multiple responses, we can evaluate each in several ways. We can give each response a score and use the score to choose which is the best response. As a final check, it is a good idea to ask ourselves whether someone we respect would feel proud of us if he or she found out we had chosen and performed a response.

SAMPLE TALLY SHEET FOR JUDGES

	Score Student 1	Score Student 2	Score Student 3	Score Student 4
First Response				
Second Response				
Third Response				

NUMBERED CARDS

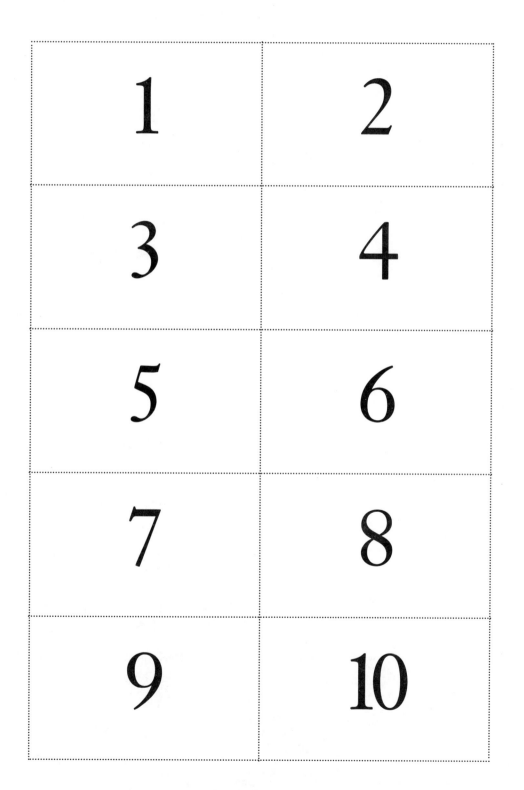

ACTIVITY SHEET 25: RESPONSE RATING FORM

WRITE your response here:

NOW, **THINK** about your response and look at each of the following statements.
Put a check in the box beside each statement that is TRUE about your response.

☐ I can identify its likely outcomes.	☐ The response deals with the problem.	☐ The response has no harmful outcome.	☐ The response helps me reach my goal(s).	☐ I am pretty sure I can carry out the response.

If you put a check mark in EVERY box, GO HERE

Now look at these statements and put a check beside each one that is true.

☐ The response is not too difficult.

☐ No surprising outcomes are likely.

IF you checked both of these boxes, give the response a score of **8 or 9.** If you are absolutely sure all these items are true, give the response a **10 (EXCELLENT).**

SCORE:

If you did NOT put a check in every box, GO HERE

Look at these statements, and put a check beside each one that is true.

☐ The response has no harmful outcome.

☐ I can identify its likely outcomes.

☐ It deals with part of the problem.

☐ It will help me reach some of my goals.

☐ I can probably carry out the response okay.

☐ The response is not too difficult.

If you checked all these boxes give the response a score of **5, 6, or 7 (Okay, but not great).**

If you gave your response a score lower than 8, think about your response. Can you change it to make it better? If so, write your new response here:

Use another sheet to score your new response.

ACTIVITY SHEET 26: ALTERNATIVE RESPONSE RATING FORM

AN EXCELLENT RESPONSE—2 STARS

IT WILL HELP ME   _____

IT WILL NOT HURT ANYONE   _____

I CAN DO IT   _____

IT WILL WORK   _____

A GOOD RESPONSE—1 STAR

IT WILL HELP ME   _____

IT WILL NOT HURT ANYONE   _____

A POOR RESPONSE—0 STARS

IT MIGHT HURT SOMEONE   _____

IT WILL NOT HELP ME   _____

Unit Summary for Group Leaders

In unit 6 we introduced several ways for children to evaluate potential responses in order to choose the most appropriate one. Students learned to identify the likely outcomes of alternative responses and to judge whether a response is helpful or harmful. They also learned to evaluate their own confidence level, that is, whether they believe they can carry out the response and it will be effective. After judging alternative responses, students learned how to choose the best response for enactment. During the course of this unit, students also had repeated opportunities to practice the first four steps in *Making Choices*. Finally, students and group leaders have begun to anticipate the conclusion of the *Making Choices* program by beginning to think about the skills they have learned and how to demonstrate these through a videotaped role play.

With completion of the fifth step in *Making Choices*, students have chosen the best response among alternatives. They are now ready to proceed to the final step in problem solving: *enactment*.

UNIT 7: ENACTMENT: ACTING ON CHOICES

The final step in *Making Choices* is *enactment*, during which children carry out the chosen response. Successful enactment often requires the ability to break down a response into a sequenced set of behaviors and to initiate this sequence in the presence of an array of distracting cues, which may be friendly, neutral, or hostile. Children must be able to complete the entire sequence while attending to situational cues that provide feedback about their success toward goals. Successful enactment often depends on a child's ability to process new information and to modify responses on the basis of new information (that is, the ability to "think on one's feet") (Crick & Dodge, 1994).

The goals of this unit are for children to enact a chosen response and to integrate all the steps of *Making Choices* in solving problems that arise in routine social situations.

The results of research indicate that children who use aggression may find it difficult to break down a response into a series of smaller steps. They are often unable to implement a sequence of behaviors in the face of the numerous stimuli present in most social situations. They appear to be especially vulnerable when encountering cues that indicate real or perceived anger in others, or cues that seem threatening. This may cause them to forget all or part of a planned response and instead to fall back on heuristic, often hostile, attribution and aggressive behavior.

In unit 7 the emphasis is on helping children integrate the material they have learned by practicing the entire *Making Choices* sequence. This unit is structured somewhat differently than previous units because little new content is introduced. Activities center on the production of a student video—or some comparable summary activity — demonstrating the six problem-solving steps. The unit's new material is presented in lesson 1, where children have the opportunity to practice breaking down a response and implementing it as a series of steps, in a variety of situations. Lesson 2 describes the process of making and taping the video. Producing a video, play, or puppet show requires multiple sessions, depending on group-specific characteristics (for example, the age, abilities, and motivation of the students). The final lesson describes a graduation ceremony, designed to bring the *Making Choices* program to a successful termination. As always, group leaders should adapt the process and content according to the needs of the students.

UNIT STRATEGY

Group leaders should encourage students to use Making Choices skills to resolve any conflicts that may arise during the design and taping of the video or during the development of an alternative activity that allows students to demonstrate problem-solving skills. Refer to the previous units, drawing on skills and phrases to reinforce the problem-solving process as it is used in developing the students' activity.

In this unit we describe the process of developing a video. The activities related to making a video are similar to those involved in developing a puppet show, a play, a rap song or opera, and other comparable activities. If it is not possible to do a video, attempt to choose an activity that requires significant interaction and that will produce a product that can be shown to parents and others. Regardless of the culminating activity, the process of creating a script, rehearsing, and giving or taping a show will produce many opportunities to use *Making Choices* skills.

Lesson 1: Enacting a Response

OBJECTIVE

Children will be able to describe a response as a series of smaller steps and will be able to implement the series of steps in a variety of situations.

Materials

- Flip chart and markers
- Situation and response ideas
- Paper and pencils

REVIEW

Check in about students' personal behavioral goals. Spend a few minutes asking whether specific *Making Choices* skills have helped them reach their goals. Why or why not?

Review the *Making Choices* steps, using an example from a previous session. Remind students that, at this point, they have chosen the best possible response and are now ready to carry it out.

ACTIVITIES

1. Refer to a simple situation from the previous session and identify the chosen response. Write it down on the flip chart. Ask for two or three volunteers to act out the situation up to the point where a response has been chosen. Stop the action and briefly review with students the steps up to this point. Then have the students continue with the role play, enacting the chosen response.

2. Ask the students to discuss the enacted response. Was the person able to carry it out? If not, why not? What were the outcomes of the response? What changed? Did it help achieve the person's goals? Why or why not?

3. Choose another situation and response. This response should be more complicated than the one used in the first activity. For example, it could involve interacting with two peers instead of one. Group leaders should prepare several situations and responses of this type beforehand. Examples might be:

- Sally is upset at Annie again because Annie ignored her at lunch. Sally decides she wants to be friends with others who aren't so snobby. She decides to call Sadie when she gets home to find out whether she wants to go to the mall.
- John is still angry at Tom for talking about his parents' argument. He has decided he wants Tom to apologize, but every time he sees Tom, Tom is with a group of other kids. John decides he needs to speak with Tom alone and tell him how he feels.

Group Process Tip: As you review previous material at the beginning of this lesson, encourage students to identify and summarize key ideas from the earlier units. Have students act out skills related to the problem-solving steps. Ask other students to provide positive feedback when someone has acted out a skill effectively. Remind students about their group rules. Be firm about not allowing put-downs or other harmful actions, and encourage members to monitor that group rules are followed.

4. Identify and write down the chosen response. Ask students to look at it closely. Can anyone describe a way to break down the response into steps of smaller actions? For example, in the situation described above, John's chosen response is that he will speak to Tom alone and tell him how he feels. He might break down the chosen response into these actions:

- When John sees Tom, he can pay attention to what Tom is doing.
- If Tom is in the middle of a game or activity, John can wait for the game to end.
- John can look around and see whether there is a good place for him to speak with Tom alone.
- John can ask himself whether he will have time to talk with Tom about how he feels.
- John can practice how he will ask Tom to talk with him alone. He can think about what he might do if Tom refuses.
- John can practice what he wants to say to Tom when they are alone.

5. Have several group members act out the situation. Group leaders should provide ample coaching and modeling (especially self-talk) and "walk through" the situation with the students. Rotate roles and make sure everyone has a chance to practice enacting one or two responses by performing a series of actions. Emphasize the idea that it is often much easier to carry out a series of simple actions when what we want to do is difficult or complex.

6. Remind students that it may be difficult to think of and remember a response when they are feeling angry or frustrated. Have students repeat the previous role plays, but instruct the second person (Tom, in the example above) to act in an unfriendly way (for example, by saying, "I don't want to talk to you—I don't want to be your friend"). Emphasize to the second person that he or she should not be too unfriendly, that is, no name calling or threatening. Have students "step out" of their roles after each role play.

7. Ask students how their ability to enact a response was affected by their feelings. Was it easier or more difficult to carry out? Why? Encourage them to use self-talk to help them stop and think whenever they are getting frustrated or angry. Repeat this exercise several times.

8. Have students draw a picture showing a response as a series of steps. Use a fairly simple response, and use paper that is divided into two or three blocks. Encourage students to break down the response on their own, but provide assistance as needed.

SUMMARIZE THE MAIN IDEA

When we wish to carry out a response, it is often helpful to break it down into a series of smaller steps. We can then carry out each small step one at a time. This can also help us carry out a response in difficult situations that make us angry or frightened.

LESSON ENRICHMENT ACTIVITY

Play a game in which students learn to break down an action into many different parts. Using an example from a previous unit, students might try to name all the separate acts involved in the action. For example, for the action "going to the cafeteria and eating lunch," these different parts might include cleaning up the work area, lining up at the door, listening to any special teacher instructions, going to the bathroom, washing hands, walking to the cafeteria, waiting while the teacher checks the mailbox at the office, lining up in the cafeteria, choosing what to eat, and so on. Group leaders might wish to encourage multiple responses by awarding a certain number of points for each response and tying points into the group's token system.

For older students, use examples of situations that are more complex and that they will find interesting. Encourage students to come up with a common social situation requiring them to carry out a moderately difficult response. For example,

A student wants to join a group of kids that she doesn't know very well in an activity. She decides to ask one of the kids if she can join.

How can she break that response down into a set of "smaller" responses?

Lesson 2: Putting It All Together—The Video

OBJECTIVE

Students will be able to demonstrate each of the six steps of the *Making Choices* program.

Materials

- Activity sheets, as needed
- Video recorder and tapes
- Paper, pencils, and crayons or markers

REVIEW

Check in with students on personal behavioral goals. Be sure to provide positive feedback for progress. Where students are making limited (or no) progress, ask the group to give constructive feedback (for example, "Is the goal important?" "Is it too difficult?" "What else might be going on?").

Review the *Making Choices* steps. Encourage students to state the steps completely on their own and to provide examples of each step, along with examples of how they can use self-talk to complete a step successfully.

ACTIVITIES

1. Explain to students that as a final project, the group will be making a video which will demonstrate appropriate problem-solving skills.

2. Group leaders should decide whether to use a situation from a previous lesson or to come up with a new one. Here we describe one way to generate a new situation in a way that actively involves all students. It may be omitted if the group is under time constraints, and group leaders can move directly to script writing activities, beginning with activity 11, below.

3. Ask students to brainstorm a list of school-related problem situations that they think would be good for taping. Group leaders should provide five or six possibilities for younger students who may not be able to generate a list. Have students vote on the top three choices.

4. Have students consider and analyze each problem by asking the following questions:

- What is the situation?
- What are the important cues and what do they mean? What is the problem? What needs to change? Who has the problem?
- What feelings might be involved?
- What goals might be helpful? Harmful?
- What responses are available to the person with the problem?
- What are the outcomes of the

Group Process Tip: This lesson may continue over more than one or two group sessions. Be sure to help students remain focused on the task at hand: producing a video tape role play (or some other group project) that demonstrates the skills they have learned. You may need to become more directive at this point in the group, to ensure that this task is completed, especially in the face of the mixed feelings students may be having about the group ending. You may want to take a few minutes at the end of the session to acknowledge these feelings. Review the material in the introduction on ending the group.

possible response?

- Which response is best? Why?
- Can the best response be broken down into a series of simple steps?

5. Review the three problems. Ask a student to summarize each situation, covering each *Making Choices* step.

6. Assign students to three groups and assign one scenario to each group. Explain to students that they will each be responsible for three drawings: one illustration depicting the situation and the problem; a second illustration showing one or two goals for the situation; and a third illustration revealing the best response and how it can be carried out.

7. Group leaders should rotate among the groups, paying attention to how students are completing this task. Encourage students to use *Making Choices* skills if they encounter problems working together as a group. As long as students are interacting productively, group leaders should not intervene. If disagreements arise—as they will— remind students to use *Making Choices* skills in solving problems.

8. When students are finished, have them present their drawings to the group. Students should explain the situation and problem in detail. They should then discuss why they formulated a particular goal, why they chose a particular response, and what they think the outcomes of the response will be.

9. Group leaders should videotape the presentations to increase students' comfort level in front of the camera.

10. Review the taped presentations as a group and then have students vote for the scenario they would like to use for the final project. Be aware of the disappointment students may feel if their situations are not chosen; provide praise and ask other students to provide praise for their hard work. Group leaders may wish to make this decision themselves, if voting is likely to cause problems. One way to decide among three equally good scenarios would be to choose one at random, perhaps by writing down each situation on a piece of paper and drawing one from a hat.

11. Review the selected scenario with students. As a large group, discuss and analyze the scenario, asking again the questions from activity 4. This will help ensure that students have encoded and interpreted all the relevant cues, formulated meaningful and attainable goals, identified multiple potential responses and considered their likely outcomes, analyzed each response in order to choose the best one, and thought about how to carry out the response as a series of simple steps.

12. Begin the process of developing the script. Use appropriate activity sheets if desired. Refer to drawings that were completed earlier as resources, if needed. The script should cover each

step of *Making Choices*. It may be helpful to think of each step as a separate act or scene. Although the length of each scene will vary, as a general rule, no scene should last longer than two or three minutes.

13. Encourage older students to write the script on their own with as little input from the group leader as possible. Younger children will need a great deal more assistance. One approach to working with young children would be to write a role play for which the group leaders take on the greater portion of the roles. Include opportunities for students to become part of the action at key points. For example, at each step you might have a student join the role play by asking him or her "to take over." With practice, even young students should be able to assume a growing role in the activities.

14. Assign roles. Try to ensure that each student has an important role. You will need the following actors: A first person, a second person, third and fourth persons (as dictated by the scenario), and a self-talker.

15. In addition, you may wish to include a narrator, who sets up the scenario by describing who is who and any background information about the characters. The narrator can explain each step of *Making Choices* before a scene begins. He or she might also "freeze the action" at critical points and explain what just happened, or ask different characters key questions about how they are feeling, what they have just done and why, or what they might do next and why.

16. Another way to include all students is to split the scenario at a key point, and develop two or more scripts. For example, at the goal formulation step, the group might come up with two different goals that are appropriate for the situation. The group leaders can assign students to two groups. Each group would perform the same script up to the goal formulation step. Then, each would develop and perform different scripts to demonstrate the subsequent steps. Some students may need the leader to be there to help and support them in carrying out their roles.

17. Begin practicing the first scene. Have several rehearsals, videotaping each one. When group leaders and students are satisfied that the scene is good enough, move to the second scene. At the end of each session, play back the scenes from that day and ask for student feedback. Make changes as needed, and make sure that the problem is clearly conveyed.

18. The final process involves putting the scenes together. Group leaders may decide to make special transitional props, such as signs that label the *Making Choices* steps or signs that help clarify what the main character is feeling, and so forth.

19. Throughout the process of taping, group leaders should provide ample praise and feedback for students. Help them remember to use self-talk and to use slogans, songs, or pantomimes whenever needed. Encourage them to praise themselves and each other.

20. During the early stages of taping, take time to have students make invitations for the final session, if it is to include the "premiere" of the videotape. Parents, family members, and teachers should be included among the guests. Students can make personalized invitations to bring home and to send to their teachers. (Food and drinks may be included as well.)

Lesson 3: Graduation and Saying Good-Bye

1. After the students have edited and completed the final product, the group should spend time planning a graduation ceremony at which the completed video will be shown to invited guests—parents, teachers, and others.

2. The graduation ceremony should include a brief description of the group and of the *Making Choices* program. (A handout outlining the process may prove useful.) Group leaders may want to help the group members prepare brief speeches stating the purpose, goals, and objectives of the program. These speeches could be presented as an introduction to the video.

3. Present each student with a certificate of recognition reflecting each child's achievements in the program.

4. Follow up: If *Making Choices* was held in a school or agency where children gather routinely, we recommend that group leaders arrange follow-up, "booster shot" discussions. These meetings should review the *Making Choices* steps and provide ample opportunity for discussion by graduates of the program. Children may use the time to share changes in their lives since the conclusion of *Making Choices*; they may talk about new friends, they may broach problems they have had with old friends, or they may have questions about using *Making Choices* skills in new circumstances. Research suggests strongly that follow up increases the effectiveness of programs like *Making Choices* (see, for example, Dishion & Andrews, 1995).

Group Process Tip: Praise students for their work in the group; review together what they've learned and the goals they have accomplished. Have students point out ways they've improved their own skills and what others have contributed to the group or class. Students should be encouraged to comment positively on how each member has changed. Help members to say good-bye to the group and to each other.

SUMMARY

The purpose of *Making Choices* is to teach social problem-solving skills to children. The program is designed for all children; however, it includes special guidelines for working with disruptive or noncompliant children. *Making Choices* is distinguished by its reliance on recent research on cognitive problem solving (especially encoding and interpretation) and by its attention to practice principles for work with children in groups. It is a carefully crafted series of lessons and activities that can be tailored for use in the classroom or with small groups.

A key element in *Making Choices* is flexibility. The practitioner, for example, is encouraged to choose activities and ways to present content so that they are culturally rich and relevant. The skills in *Making Choices* are building blocks for sustaining satisfying relationships with others—both peers and adults—and for working cooperatively in school and employment settings. These skills include the ability to assess the social environment, to select context-sensitive goals that strengthen relationships with others, and to carry out activities in a harmonious way.

Regardless of the group's composition—for example, a class of third-grade students or a small group of oppositional "high-risk" first-grade boys—*Making Choices* should be provided in settings where the balance of children are not viewed as at-risk for problem behavior. The roots of *Making Choices* lie in our growing understanding of prosocial behavior. To promote prosocial behavior, it is highly desirable that *Making Choices* be used in a setting in which the majority of children do not have conduct problems.

In our own work, we have tested *Making Choices* in third- and sixth-grade classrooms where it is delivered to all children, some of whom have relational problems but most of whom do not. We are also in the process of testing *Making Choices* in after-school programs operated by churches, Boys and Girls Clubs, YMCAs, and public schools. In these after-school settings, a mixed group format is used. Here, groups are set up such that children with developmentally appropriate social skills always constitute a majority. We have found that this keeps group discussion positive, it gives leadership opportunities to prosocial children, and it helps to break down the peer rejection that is the source of problem behavior in some children.[1]

When *Making Choices* is used with children who have serious conduct problems, it should be combined with other services that address the range of risk factors that influence problem behavior (for a review, see Fraser, 1997). These usually include individual, family, school, and neighborhood influences. We have developed a complementary program, called *Strong Families*, that addresses family-related risk factors for conduct problems. This curriculum is currently being tested and refined.

It is representative of one type of program that might be added to a multielement strategy aimed at addressing family risk factors (for example, inconsistent discipline), school risk factors (inadequate support, for example), and neighborhood risk factors (unsafe streets to and from school, for example).

The bottom line: *Making Choices* is by itself only one of many potential programs that might be marshaled to strengthen services for children. Recent research suggests that a multielement intervention does not need to address all of the potential risk factors affecting children to have a significant effect. It should, however, address the keystone or major factors that put children at-risk (Fraser & Galinsky,1997), and *Making Choices* is designed to address two keystone factors—poor social skills and peer rejection—that affect many children.

We hope that you will find *Making Choices* useful in working with children. We continue to make refinements in the content of *Making Choices*, and we invite your comments and contributions. If you develop a lesson that you think other group leaders might want to use, please send a copy to us.

Finally, we offer special thanks to all of the practitioners, parents, and children who have contributed to the development of the *Making Choices* program.

---

[1] Moreover, some research suggests that creating groups composed entirely of children at risk may do more harm than good (Dishion & Andrews, 1995; Feldman et al., 1983). Groups composed entirely of children with problems inevitably create opportunities for more disruptive children to incite less disruptive children. Occasionally, too, more disruptive children model more extreme forms of problem behavior for less disruptive children. In some settings, such as residential treatment programs and group homes, it is not possible to provide services to children who are not at-risk in some way. However, such programs are often able to create mixed groups comprising more settled resident children and newer resident children who may still be reacting to recent negative life experiences. In short, *Making Choices* groups should, whenever possible, include a diverse group of children. The mixed group structure provides opportunities for leadership, it reduces labeling effects, it ensures that groups will have a prosocial perspective, and it encourages the formation of positive peer relationships.

REFERENCES

Bandura, A. (1993). Perceived self-efficacy in cognitive development and functioning. *Educational Psychologist, 28*(2), 117-148.

Bloomquist, M. L. (1996). *Skills training for children with behavior disorders: A parent and therapist guidebook.* New York: Guilford Press.

Branden-Muller, L. R., Elias, M. J., Gara, M. A., & Schneider, K. (1992). The development and interrelationship of affective, cognitive, and social-cognitive skills in children: Theoretical implications. *Journal of Applied Developmental Psychology, 13,* 271-291.

Brower, A. M. (1996). Group development as constructed social reality revisited: The constructivism of small groups. *Families in Society, 77,* 336-344.

Brower, A. M., & Nurius, P. S. (1993). *Social cognition and individual change: Current theory and counseling guidelines.* Newbury Park, CA: Sage Publications.

Cartledge, G., Lee, J. W., & Feng, H. (1995). Cultural diversity: Multicultural factors in teaching social skills. In G. Cartledge & J. F. Milburn (Eds.), *Teaching social skills to children and youth: Innovative approaches* (3rd ed., pp. 328-355). Boston: Allyn & Bacon.

Crick, N. R. (1995). Relational aggression: The role of intent attributions, feelings of distress, and provocation type. *Development and Psychopathology, 7,* 313-322.

Crick, N. R. (1996). The role of overt aggression, relational aggression, and prosocial behavior in the prediction of children's future social adjustment. *Child Development, 67,* 2317-2327.

Crick, N. R., & Dodge, K. A. (1994). A review and reformulation of social-information processing mechanisms in children's social adjustment. *Psychological Bulletin, 115*(1), 74-101.

Crick, N. R., & Grotpeter, J. K. (1995). Relational aggression, gender, and social-psychological adjustment. *Child Development, 66,* 710-722.

Crick, N. R., & Grotpeter, J. K. (1996). Children's treatment by peers: Victims of relational and overt aggression. *Development and Psychopathology, 8,* 367-380.

Crick, N. R., & Wellman, N. E. (1997). Response decision processes in relational and overt aggression. Unpublished manuscript.

Dawes, R. M. (1988). *Rational choice in an uncertain world.* Fort Worth, TX: Harcourt Brace College Publishers.

Dishion, T. J., & Andrews, D. W. (1995). Preventing escalation in problem behaviors with high-risk young adolescents: Immediate and 1-year outcomes. *Journal of Clinical and Consulting Psychology, 63,* 538-548.

Dodge, K. A., Bates, J. E., & Pettit, G. S. (1990). Mechanisms in the cycle of violence. *Science, 250,* 1678-1683.

Dodge, K. A., Pettit, J. E., Bates, G. S., & Valente, E. (1995). Social information-processing patterns partially mediate the effect of early physical abuse on later conduct problems. *Journal of Abnormal Psychology, 104,* 632-643.

Dodge, K. A., Price, J. M., Bachorowski, J., & Newman, J. P. (1990). Hostile attribution biases in severely aggressive adolescents. *Journal of Abnormal Psychology, 99,* 385-392.

Feldman, R. A., Caplinger, T. E., & Wodarski, J. S. (1983). *The St. Louis Conundrum: The effective treatment of antisocial youths.* Englewood Cliffs, NJ: Prentice Hall.

Fraser, M. W. (1996a). Aggressive behavior in childhood and early adolescence: An ecological-developmental perspective on youth violence. *Social Work, 41,* 347-361.

Fraser, M. W. (1996b). Cognitive problem-solving and aggressive behavior among children. *Families in Society: The Journal of Contemporary Human Services, 71*(1), 19-32.

Fraser, M. W. (Ed.). (1997). Risk and resilience in childhood: An ecological perspective. Washington DC: NASW Press.

Fraser, M. W., & Galinsky, M. J. (1997). Toward a resilience-based model of practice. In Fraser, M. W. (Ed.), Risk and resilience in childhood: perspective (pp. 265–275). Washington DC: NASW Press.

Galinsky, M. J., & Schopler, J. H. (1989). Developmental patterns in open-ended groups. *Social Work with Groups, 12*(2), 99-114.

Garland, J. A., Jones, H. E., & Kolodny, R. L. (1976). A model for stages of development in social work groups. In S. Bernstein (Ed.), *Explorations in group work* (pp. 17-72). Boston: Boston University School of Social Work.

Garvin, C. (1997). *Contemporary group work* (3rd ed.). Boston: Allyn & Bacon.

Goldstein, A. P. (1988). *The prepare curriculum.* Champaign, IL: Research Press.

Gouze, K. R. (1987). Attention and social problem-solving as correlates of aggression in preschool males. *Journal of Abnormal Child Psychology, 15*, 181-197.

Graham, S., Hudley, C., & Williams, E. (1992). Attributional and emotional determinants of aggression among African-American and Latino young adolescents. *Developmental Psychology, 28*, 731-740.

Grossman, D., Neckerman, H., Koepsell, T., Liu, P., Asher, K., Beland, K., Frey, K., & Rivara, F. (1997). Effectiveness of a violence prevention curriculum among children in elementary school: A randomized controlled trial. *JAMA, 277*, 1605-1611.

Guerra, N. G., Tolan, P. H., Huesmann, L. R., Van Acker, R., & Eron, L. D. (1995). Stressful events and individual beliefs as correlates of economic disadvantage and aggression among urban children. *Journal of Consulting and Clinical Psychology, 63*, 518-528.

Hughes, J. N., & Cavell, T. A. (1995). Cognitive-affective approaches: Enhancing competence in aggressive children. In G. Cartledge & J. F. Milburn (Eds.), *Teaching social skills to children and youth* (3rd ed., pp. 199-236). Boston: Allyn & Bacon.

Kelly, T. B., & Berman-Rossi, T. (1999). Advancing stages of group development theory: The case of institutionalized older persons. *Social Work with Groups, 22*(2/3), 119–138.

Kendall, P. C. (1993). Cognitive-behavioral therapies with youth: Guiding theory, current status, and emerging developments. *Journal of Consulting and Clinical Psychology, 61*, 235-247.

Ladd, G. W., & Price, J. M. (1986). Promoting children's cognitive and social competence: The relation between parents' perceptions of task difficulty and children's perceived and actual competence. *Child Development, 57*, 446-460.

Larson, J. (1994). Cognitive-behavioral treatment of anger-induced aggression in the school setting. In M. Furlong & D. Smith (Eds.), *Anger, hostility, and aggression: Assessment, prevention, and intervention strategies for youth* (pp. 393-440). Brandon, VT: Clinical Psychology Publishing Co.

Lochman, J. E. (1992). Cognitive-behavioral intervention with aggressive boys: Three-year follow-up and preventive effects. *Journal of Consulting and Clinical Psychology, 60*, 426-432.

Lochman, J. E., Coie, J. D., Underwood, M. K., & Terry, R. (1993). Effectiveness of a social relations intervention program for aggressive and nonaggressive, rejected children. *Journal of Consulting and Clinical Psychology, 61*, 1053-1058.

Lochman, J. E., & Dodge, K. A. (1994). Social-cognitive processes of severely violent, moderately aggressive, and nonaggressive boys. *Journal of Consulting and Clinical Psychology, 62*, 366-374.

Lochman, J. E., Dunn, S. E., & Klimes-Dougan, B. (1993). An intervention and consultation model from a social cognitive perspective: A description of the anger coping program. *School Psychology Review, 22,* 458-471.

Lochman, J. E., Lampron, L. B., Gemmer, T. C., & Harris, S. R. (1987). Anger coping intervention with aggressive children: A guide to implementation in school settings. In P. A. Keller & S. R. Heyman (Eds.), *Innovations in clinical practice: A source book* (Vol. 6, pp. 339-355). Sarasota, FL: Professional Resource Exchange.

Lochman, J. E., & Lenhart, L. A. (1993). Anger coping intervention for aggressive children: Conceptual models and outcome effects. *Clinical Psychology Review, 13,* 785-805.

Milich, R., & Dodge, K. A. (1984). Social information processing in child psychiatric populations. *Journal of Abnormal Child Psychology, 12,* 471-490.

Nurius, P. S., & Berlin, S. B. (1995). Cognition and social cognitive theory. In R. L. Edwards (Ed. in-Chief), *Encyclopedia of social work* (19 ed., Vol. 1, pp. 513-524). Washington, DC: NASW Press.

Perry, D. G., Perry, L. C., & Rasmussen, P. (1986). Cognitive social learning mediators of aggression. *Child Development, 57,* 700-711.

Pettit, G. S., Dodge, K. A., & Brown, M. M. (1988). Early family experience, social problem-solving patterns, and children's social competence. *Child Development, 59,* 107-120.

Quiggle, N. L., Garber, J., Panak, W. F., & Dodge, K. A. (1992). Social information processing in aggressive and depressed children. *Child Development, 63,* 1305-1320.

Rabiner, D., & Coie, J. (1989). Effect of expectancy inductions on rejected children's acceptance by unfamiliar peers. *Developmental Psychology, 25,* 450-457.

Rabiner, D. L., Lenhart, L., & Lochman, J. E. (1990). Automatic versus reflective social problem-solving in relation to children's sociometric status. *Developmental Psychology, 26,* 1010-1016.

Rose, S. D. (1998). *Group therapy with troubled youth: A cognitive-behavioral interactive approach.* Thousand Oaks, CA: Sage Publications.

Sarri, R. C., & Galinsky, M. J. (1985). A conceptual framework for group development. In M. Sundel, P. Glasser, R. Sarri, & R. Vinter (Eds.), *Individual change through small groups* (2nd ed., pp. 70-86). New York: Free Press.

Sheline, J. L., Skipper, B. J., & Broadhead, W. E. (1994). Risk factors for violent behavior in elementary school boys: Have you hugged your child today? *American Journal of Public Health, 84,* 661-663.

Slaby, R. G., & Guerra, N. G. (1988). Cognitive mediators of aggression in adolescent offenders: 1. Assessment. *Developmental Psychology, 24,* 580-588.

Tolan, P. H., Guerra, N. G., & Kendall, P. C. (1995). A developmental-ecological perspective on antisocial behavior in children and adolescents: Toward a unified risk and intervention framework. *Journal of Consulting and Clinical Psychology, 63,* 579-584.

Toseland, R. W., & Rivas, R. F. (1998). *An introduction to group work practice* (3rd ed.). Boston: Allyn & Bacon.

Tuckman, B. W., & Jensen, M. A. (1977). Stages of small group development revisited. *Group and Organization Studies, 2,* 419-427.

Tversky, A., & Kahneman, D. (1983). Extensional versus intuitive reasoning: the conjunction fallacy in probability judgment. *Psychological Review, 90,* 293-315.

Wheelan, S. A., & Kaeser, R. M. (1997). The influence of task type and designated leaders on developmental patterns in groups. *Small Group Research, 28,* 94-121.

Worchel, S. (1994). You can go home again: Returning group research to the group context with an eye on developmental issues. *Small Group Research, 25,* 205-223.

APPENDIX: TABLES AND FIGURES

TABLE 1: SOCIAL INFORMATION-PROCESSING

Steps in Social Information-Processing Sequence	Activities and Requisite Skills
1. Encoding of cues	*Encoding* involves recognizing and reading the numerous cues encountered in social situations and, from the wide range of cues present, selecting those cues that are relevant and significant. A child must be able to perceive and attend to contextual cues as well as to cues flowing from others (verbal and physical), and to distinguish subtle nuances and sequences of cues.
2. Interpretation of cues	*Interpretation* refers to the process by which children assign meaning to social cues. It involves assessing cues from the current social situation, drawing from previous experiences (including earlier social interactions, past relationships, prior exposure to similar situations, and so on) and from the ability to recognize and interpret the context in which cues appear. A child brings to bear both prior knowledge and interpretive skills in making sense of novel situations. Attribution of others' intentions is a critical component of assigning meaning to social cues. The ability to assess social cues accurately is essential for creating and implementing an effective social strategy.
3. Goal formulation	*Goal formulation* involves developing a focused awareness of desired outcomes to guide action. This process is shaped by cultural norms, past experiences, socialization, modeling, and emotional stability. Desired outcomes may reflect aspirations for material goods (a new CD, for example) or meet affective needs (to be happy or to feel self worth, for example). Development of prosocial goals requires that children value positive interpersonal relationships (over, for example, establishing dominance). During this process, it is important that children have the ability to conceptualize multiple goals, to evaluate competing goals, and to distinguish short- and long-term goals.

TABLE 1: SOCIAL INFORMATION-PROCESSING (CONTINUED)

Steps in Social Information-Processing Sequence	Activities and Requisite Skills
4. Response search and formulation	*Response search and formulation* refers to a child's ability to identify multiple potential responses in a social situation. It may involve accessing responses from memory (that is, ones that have been used in previous situations), constructing new responses, or both. In order to interact with others in a prosocial manner and in a variety of social situations, children need to be able to access a wide array of potential responses from which to choose an appropriate one. During this step, children must be able to keep in mind their goal for the situation.
5. Response decision	The fifth step in the cognitive problem-solving sequence is *response decision*. This is the point at which the child reviews all potential response options and selects the one option that best fits the given situation or problem. An adequate response should correspond well to desired goal and to the current situation. Critical factors in response decision are: (1) the child's degree of confidence that he or she is capable of enacting a selected response, and (2) the child's assessment of the likelihood that the response will be effective in bringing about the desired outcomes.
6. Enactment	During *enactment*, the child carries out the selected response. Several factors, such as the child's ability to break down a response into a sequence of steps, the appropriateness of the response with respect to the situation and goals, and the degree to which flexibility is built into the response, may influence the likelihood of success.

SOURCE: Crick, N. R., & Dodge, K. A. (1994). A review and reformulation of social-information processing mechanisms in children's social adjustment. *Psychological Bulletin*, 115(1), 74-101.

FIGURE 1: PERSPECTIVES ON BEHAVIOR

Behavioral Approach

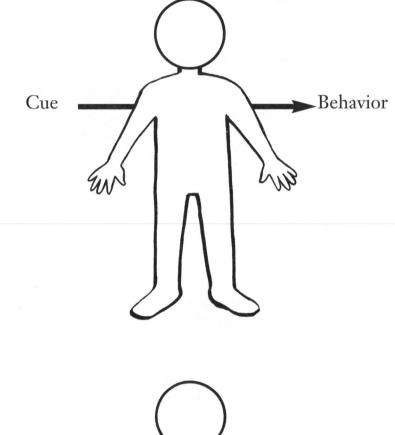

Cue → Behavior

Social-Cognitive Approach

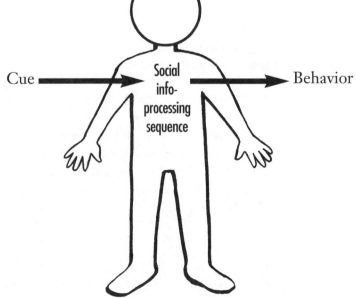

Cue → Social info-processing sequence → Behavior

FIGURE 2: SINGLE SOCIAL INFORMATION-PROCESSING SEQUENCE

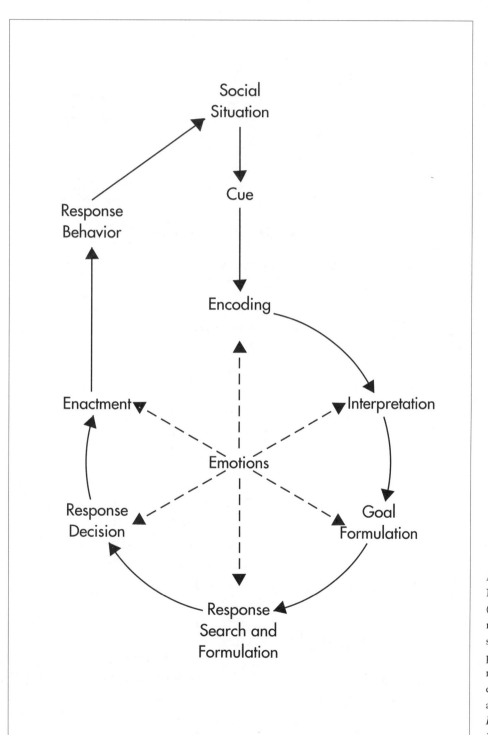

Adapted from: Crick, N. R., & Dodge, K. A. (1994). A review and reformulation of social-information processing mechanisms in children's social adjustment. *Psychological Bulletin*, 115 (1), 74-101.

FIGURE 3: THE AVAILABILITY HEURISTIC AND INTERPRETATION

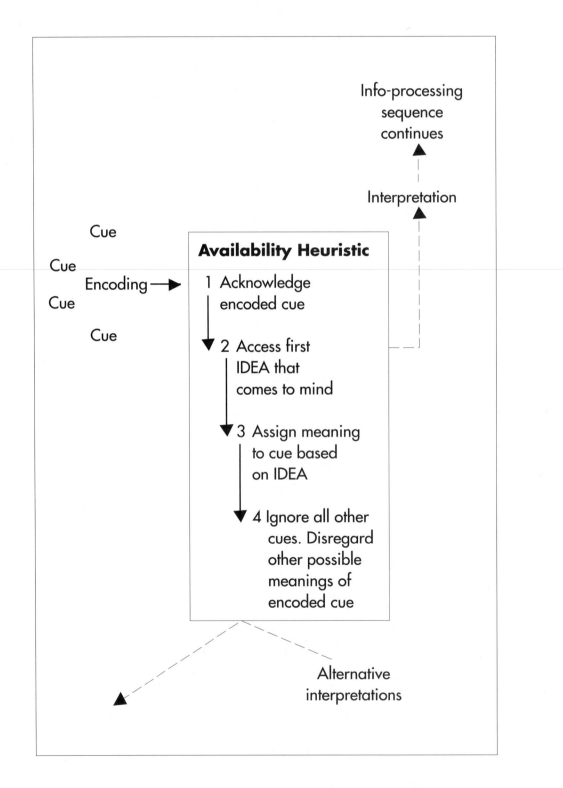

FIGURE 4 AND 4A: *MAKING CHOICES* **PROBLEM SOLVING "STAIRCASE"**

FIGURE 4

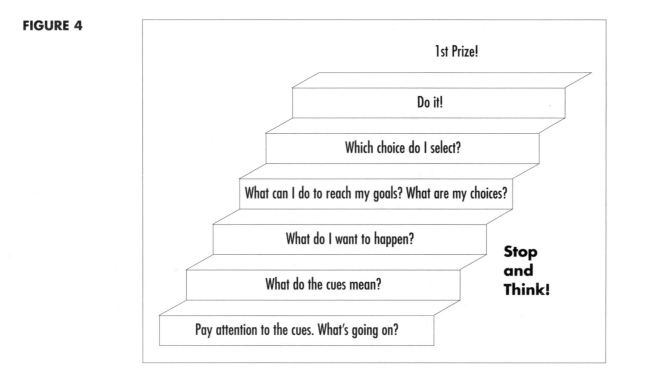

FIGURE 4A

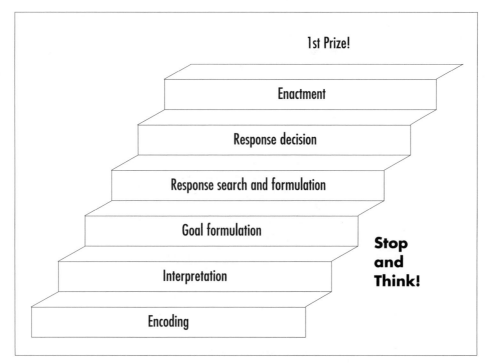

INDEX

CRITICAL NASW PRESS RESOURCES FOR YOUR PRACTICE WITH CHILDREN, YOUTHS, AND FAMILIES

Making Choices: Social Problem-Solving Skills for Children, *Mark W. Fraser, James K. Nash, Maeda J. Galinsky, and Kathleen M. Darwin.* (The first volume in the NASW Practice Resources Series.) Based on a cognitive problem-solving approach, *Making Choices* addresses the urgent need for children to acquire competence in meeting the demands of childhood within social, school, and family parameters. The book is designed for children from kindergarten through middle school whose behavior is impulsive, oppositional, or aggressive. Recognizing that a great deal of children's behavior is tied to problem-solving, the volume focuses on how children solve instrumental and relational issues in differing social settings.

ISBN: 0-87101-323-1. Item #3231. $33.99.

Youth Violence: *Current Research and Recent Practice Innovations, Jeffrey M. Jenson and Matthew O. Howard, Editors.* A timely, eye-opening book on the youth violence that has galvanized the nation. *Youth Violence* pinpoints and probes the etiology of this escalating trend, which is found in urban, suburban, and rural contexts. The authors analyze five types of youth violence—child abuse and violence, aggression among girls, school violence, substance abuse and violence, and gang violence.

ISBN: 0-87101-311-8. Item #3118. $35.95.

Multisystem Skills and Interventions in School Social Work Practice, *Edith M. Freeman, Cynthia G. Franklin, Rowena Fong, Gary L. Shaffer, and Elizabeth M. Timberlake, Editors.* This is a practical guide that will help you meet the emerging needs of students, families, schools, and communities today. You'll learn about the skills and competencies you need to work effectively with new social work consumers. And you'll find out how you can change policies, gain funding, and otherwise influence large systems in the changing socio-political climate.

ISBN: 0-87101-295-2. Item #2952. $29.95.

Clinical Practice with Individuals, *by Mark A. Mattaini.* Practitioners and educators alike will find this guidebook invaluable. It provides clear guidelines to help practitioners identify key factors operating in particular cases and create new interventions when needed. The ecobehavioral approach Mattaini outlines can be very effective in short-term treatment.

ISBN: 0-87101-270-7. Item #2707. $28.95.

Clinical Intervention with Families, *by Mark A. Mattaini.* (companion volume to *Clinical Practice with Individuals*). Written for social workers in family practice as well as for instructors and advanced-level students, this book is a state-of-the-art and state-of-the-science treatment guide of family practice. An essential volume for those seeking to understand the extrinsic family factors affecting the theory and practice of family social work!

ISBN: 0-87101-308-8. Item #3088. $32.95.

Risk and Resilience in Childhood: *An Ecological Perspective, Mark W. Fraser, Editor.* How is it that some children face enormous odds but prevail over adversity to become successful? How can you develop practice models that foster resilience? You'll find answers to these questions and more in this unique text that introduces and explores the concepts of protection and resilience in the face of adversity.

ISBN: 0-87101-274-X. Item #274X. $35.95.

(Order form on reverse side)

ORDER FORM

Qty.	Title	Item #	Price	Total
__	Making Choices	3231	$33.99	_____
__	Youth Violence	3118	$35.95	_____
__	Multisystem Skills and Interventions in School SW Practice	2952	$29.95	_____
__	Clinical Practice with Individuals	2707	$28.95	_____
__	Clinical Intervention with Families	3088	$32.95	_____
__	Risk and Resilience in Childhood	274X	$35.95	_____

Subtotal	_____
Postage and Handling	_____
DC residents add 6% sales tax	_____
MD residents add 5% sales tax	_____
Total	_____

POSTAGE AND HANDLING
Minimum postage and handling fee is $4.95.
Orders that do not include appropriate
postage and handling will be returned.

DOMESTIC: Please add 12% to orders under
$100 for postage and handling. For orders
over $100 add 7% of order.

CANADA: Please add 17% postage and
handling.

OTHER INTERNATIONAL: Please add 22%
postage and handling.

❑ **Check** or **money order** (payable to NASW Press) for $ _____.

❑ **Credit card**
  ❑ NASW Visa* | ❑ Visa | ❑ NASW MasterCard* | ❑ MasterCard | ❑ Amex

_____   _____
Credit Card Number   Expiration Date

Signature _____

Use of these cards generates funds in support of the social work profession.

Name _____

Address _____

City _____ State/Province _____

Country _____ Zip _____

Phone _____ E-mail _____

NASW Member # (if applicable) _____

(Please make checks payable to NASW Press. Prices are subject to change.)

NASW PRESS
P. O. Box 431
Annapolis JCT, MD 20701
USA

Credit card orders call
1-800-227-3590
(In the Metro Wash., DC, area, call 301-317-8688)
Or fax your order to 301-206-7989
Or order online at http://www.naswpress.org

Visit our Web site at http://www.naswpress.org.   MC900